Alice Harvey
with much affection
from the author
Louise Redington Peirson

THE GARDEN WAY
FROM
EAST TO WEST

THE GARDEN WAY
FROM EAST TO WEST

BY

LOUISE REDINGTON PIERSON

Transcript Printing Company
Peterborough, N. H.
1934

COPYRIGHTED
1934
LOUISE REDINGTON PIERSON

PRINTED IN U. S. A.

ACKNOWLEDGMENTS

To the following people: For the help received in the writing of this book, I wish to express my gratitude: To Miss Mary Adams for her kindly criticism and encouragement in the early stages of creation, when she put into practice the maxim of Horace "Begin with Truth, then give Invention Scope."

To Mrs. Alison B. Alessios, of the New York Public Library, whose knowledge and untiring effort smoothed the way of a novice in the details of book manufacture; whose sympathy and persistent encouragement have finally brought to completion this little volume.

To Monsignor Joseph M. McMahon for his careful criticism of the chapter "The Path to the Cloister."

To the librarians in the Boston Public Library, and the special library of the Boston Fine Arts for their kindly help in finding books, from which notes were taken, unfortunately without recording the titles or authors before I thought of publishing the book. To these unrecorded authors, I present my apologies and gratitude.

To the proof readers and publisher for their interest and labor in behalf of the book.

To the following publishers for permission to quote from copyright material:

To Messrs. E. P. Dutton & Company for use of "Epode II." by Horace (Every Man's Library); for numerous passages from the "History of Garden Art" by Marie Luise Gothein, a book so full of valuable information delightfully told, I would be glad if my little volume might serve as its introduction to garden lovers not already familiar with it.

ACKNOWLEDGMENTS

To Messrs. Macmillan & Co. for the use of material in "Greek Studies" by Walter Pater; for the use of material in the Introduction to the poems of Theocritus and translation of "Idyll VII." by Andrew Lang; for material from "Song and Its Fountains" by A. E.; for quotations from "Seven Ages of Washington" by Owen Wister.

To Messrs G. P. Putnam's Sons for the use of poems by Poliziana and Lorenzo di Medici from "Lorenzo the Magnificent" by Horsburg; "The Way of St. James" by Georgiana Goddard King; for material from "Life of Akhnaton" by Arthur Weigall.

To Messrs. Little, Brown & Company for material from "In and Out of the Old Missions of California" by George Wharton James.

To Robert McBride and Company for use of material from "Tamerlaine" by Harold Lamb; for material from "Garden Cities of Old Mexico" by James F. Jenkins in the May number 1933 of "Travel."

To Charles Scribner and Sons, for the use of a quotation from "The Apostolic Age" by A. C. McGiffert; for the use of two letters from "Letters of Eliza Lucas Pinkney" by Harriott Hovey Ravenal.

To the Viking Press for the use of material from "The Power and Secret of the Jesuits" by Rene Tulop-Miller.

To the Oxford University Press for material from the "Odyssey" translated by J. E. Shaw.

To Longmans Green and Company for material from "Curious Myths of the Middle Ages" by S. Baring Gould.

In addition to books from which quotations have been taken are,

General histories, encyclopedias, magazine articles. A Child's History of the World by V. M. Hillyer published

ACKNOWLEDGMENTS

by Century Co. History of Egypt by J. H. Breasted, published by Hodder. History of Egypt by Wallis Budge, published by G. P. Putnam's Sons. Life of Akhnaton by Arthur Weigall, published by G. P. Putnam's Sons. Greek Studies by Walter Pater, published by Macmillan Co. Marius The Epicurean by Walter Pater, published by Macmillan Co. History of Rome by Ferraro Guglielmo. Italy in the Thirteenth Century by Henry D. Sedwick, published by Houghton-Mifflin Co. The Thirteenth, the Greatest of Centuries by J. J. Wright, published by Catholic Summer Press. Scenes and Characters of the Middle Ages by E. L. Cutts, published by Simkin Marshall Hamilton, Kent & Co., London. St. Francis of Assisi by Father Cuthbert, published by Longmans Green & Co. St. Francis of Assisi by Jorgensen, translated by T. O. Connor Sloan, published by Longmans Green & Co. Italian Villas by Edith Wharton, published by the Century Co. Italian Backgrounds by Edith Wharton, published by Charles Scribner & Sons. Medici by G. F. Young, published by E. P. Dutton & Co. The Alhambra, published by G. P. Putnam's Sons. Life of Columbus and Companions by Washington Irving, published by G. P. Putnam's Sons. Gardens of Spain and Portugal by Rose Standish Nichols. Mudéjar by Georgiana Goddard King (Bryn Mawr Monographs), published by Longmans Green & Co. Gardens by J. C. N. Forestier, published by Charles Scribner's Sons. Chinese Paintings by John C. Ferguson, published by the University of Chicago. The Scented Garden by Eleanor Sinclair Rohde, published by Hale Cushman & Flint. The Divine Comedy by Dante. The Bible.

To my Sister

*through the open gates of whose garden
have come many visions
of beauty*

CONTENTS

CHAPTER		PAGE
I.	Among the Orientals	1
II.	Among the Greeks	17
III.	Among the Romans	35
IV.	A Path to the Cloister	47
V.	A Path of Romance and Poetry	73
VI.	A Path in Moorish Spain	93
VII.	A Path of the Adventurer	113
VIII.	A Path from West to East	143

THE study of garden history is a fascinating one. It carries us far afield, showing how important in the history of the world gardens are.

Agriculture is the back-bone of all civilization. Life is dependent on the garden, a place set apart for growing living things,—all depending on earth, air, fire, and water,— gifts of the deity, Pagan or Christian. Many paths lead to the garden. From the north comes the path of science, throwing light on the workings of nature, but still the mystery of life remains a secret. To the west lies the path of adventure ever following the sun around the world in search of the treasure house of the East. Between East and West lies the Southland, the home of imagination and poetry.

History begins with a myth. Myth begins with a dream, the dream becomes real, nature takes on a personality. Sun, moon, land, and water, are deities; animals become their symbols.

Let us enter the realm of Dream and Fancy.

CHAPTER I

AMONG THE ORIENTALS

"There was never mystery
But 'tis figured in the flowers."

EMERSON

CHAPTER I

A COUNTRY particularly adapted to dream life is Egypt. The long, narrow strip of land, fertilized by the Nile, runs north and south; on the east and west stretch great deserts, out of one of which the sun appears to rise, and floating majestically through the sky, to fall mysteriously into another beyond the known realm. To the Egyptian it is the Sun God. Adventurous spirits eager to reach the rising and setting of this glorious creature, floating daily over their land, find, after weary traveling on their faithful camels, that their god comes up out of one sea and drops into another that surround the deserts.

A dreamer sees a cloud pass over the sun, transforming it, to him, into a boat with bulging sail; and to his imaginative mind, it carries the sun god over his kingdom every day. An artist has perpetuated the dream in the exquisite low reliefs in the temple of Abydos.

In prehistoric days Heliopolis was the great city of Egypt for the worship of Atum, the Sun God. No remains of these days have survived except tradition. Fortunately that has survived through literature and paintings preserved in the tombs and pyramids.

Contemporary with the Egyptian civilization was the Babylonian, and back of them stretched a long tradition of agricultural people whose story is now being dug up by archaeologists. Professor Wooley, in a delightful little book, tells us of the Sumerians struggling with Semite and Hittite for the possession of the land from the Persian Gulf to the mountains beyond the Tigris and the high plateau of Syria to the West. It was a wonderfully fertile country and tempting to settlers, among whom the Sumerians were the first to develop a civilization. According to the account in Genesis, they apparently were "the people who journeyed from the east and came into the plains of Shinar and dwelt there." Professor Wooley tells us that they spread up the valleys of the Tigris and Euphrates, into Syria and even into Asia beyond the Taurus, carrying with them a civilization that is the inheritance of the world.

While Egyptian history, according to Greek tradition, began with Menes in the third millennium B. C., old inscriptions refer to the country as two lands, the North and the South. Menes united them and moved his capital to Memphis, making Ptah, the local God of the Craftsmen, the god of both north and south, and gave to him many of the attributes of Atum, the sun god of Heliopolis.

The high and mighty ones of Memphis were buried in the desert in sumptuous tombs decorated with truly beautiful wall paintings in such splendid preservation today, that we can study there the story of a happy agricultural life. Long processions of laborers bring the fruits of the earth; flowers, herbs and flocks for the nobles' use in the new life into which they are about to enter. Death is not pictured in the ancient tombs of Sakkarah. Immortality is firmly believed in, at least for the King and his nobles. Pyramid texts are full of emotional appeals to the sun god to receive the spirits of the high and mighty into the realm of the sun. Some believed that the dead became stars, and the doors of the pyramids in many cases faced the north, so that the spirit could fly directly to the sky, especially the region of the polar star. An early symbol of immortality was the winged hawk placed on the pyramid.

One of the great mysteries of the Egyptian world was the annual inundation of the Nile, bringing the return of life to the parched land. This mystery was personified in the person of Osiris, an offspring of the sun god and the earth mother. Osiris was supposed to have reigned as king on the earth, and to have brought the tribe out of savagery by wise laws. He and his sister-queen, Isis, discovered wheat and barley growing wild, which they cultivated, thus bringing wealth to their people. They also taught the use of fruit and the making of wine. In the course of time they became the gods of the nether world, into which the spirits of the dead must enter that their hearts might be weighed and their lives judged. If found worthy they could journey on until they reached a paradise of verdure. Osiris was also supposed to have taught the worship of the gods.

Out of this welter of mythology stretches a long line of real personages through the ages. The first to leave a record of garden art, as far as we know, is Queen Hatshepsut, who in 1600 B. C., built her palaces and temples on terraces with gardens about them at Deir-el-Bakhari. In a corridor at the back of the highest, the story of her deeds is told in words and pictures. How the god Amon [of Thebes] bade her make at his house a garden so large that he could walk therein. She must fetch incense trees from the land of Punt, the country of the gods, where many trees grew. There the Queen's people collected all sorts of treasures for the god's garden, and brought them home and planted them in the pleasure garden of Amon.* Among the trees, brought from Punt, especially valued for their shade, fruit and wood, were figs, pomegranates, and sycamores.

According to an ancient tradition the sycamore was set beside the rising and the setting sun. It is also re-

---

*Professor Breasted gives a delightful description of the expedition in his history of Egypt, chap. xv., p. 278.

garded as the friend of lovers, and every year a festival is held in its honor, when it is in the full glory of its flowering.

Probably the following poem is the earliest one written in honor of any tree:

> The little sycamore
> Which she planted with her own hand,
> She moves her lips to speak—
> How fair are her lovely branches:
> She is laden with fruits
> That are redder than the jasper—
> Her shade is cool.
> She lays a little letter in a girl's hand,
> The head gardener's daughter—
> She bids her hasten to the well-beloved:
> Come and stay among the maidens.
> We are drunken if we would go to thee,
> Ay, before we have tasted aught—
> The servants who obey thee
> Are coming with their vessels;
> Wine of every kind they bring,
> And every kind of bread,
> Many flowers of today and yesterday
> And all refreshing fruits—
> Come, and make it fine today,
> Tomorrow and next day three days long—
> Sit in my shade.*

It is the spring of the year in Egypt. From Gilead comes a caravan of traders, their camels laden with spices, balm and myrrh. They bring with them a Syrian lad, Joseph, sold to them on the way. Potipher, an officer of the Pharaoh, buys him and he becomes a part of the royal household at Thebes. We may imagine that this happened in the reign of Amenophis III., whose wife was the celebrated Queen Tiy, daughter of a Syrian chief Yuan, and Tuan, his wife.

---

*History of Art of Garden-Making. Marie Luise Gothein. By courtesy of E. P. Dutton Co.

Naturally Queen Tiy would take an interest in the clever lad from her father's country, and be glad to have him the companion of her only son, the delicate Amenophis IV.

The palace at Thebes occupied a superb site high above the Nile under cliffs of marvellous color, changing every hour of the day. The walls of the palace were painted with scenes of animal life, wild cattle running through swamps, pigeons flying overhead; and through curtained doorways came glimpses of the gardens filled with gay flowers, foreign to Egypt. Beyond the gardens in the midst of trees brought from Asia shone the great pleasure lake.

Pictures show the typical Egyptian garden surrounded with high walls, and the dwelling hidden by trees. There is a pond with green border where water fowl enliven the scene, a vineyard with different kinds of trees in straight avenues—a rectangular form symbolizing the four essentials. . . .

The entrance gate leads straight into the garden, from whence the visitors proceed to the house where, in an open porch, they are received. A pergola near by is covered with grape vines.

There in the gardens the boys would play. Surrounded with such beauty, the mind of the delicate little Pharaoh-to-be early in life learned to love nature in her various moods. Queen Tiy was a woman of power and ability, and when her husband died, she took the reins of government into her own hands during the long minority of her son.

Amenophis IV. inherited from his father a dreamy nature, and it does not require a great deal of imagination to picture Joseph telling his dreams to the young Pharaoh, and bragging that his people worshipped the

Power that made the sun, while the Egyptians worshipped only the sun. Amenophis would ask if Joseph's people had beautiful temples with gardens and ponds full of lotus-flowers around them, and Joseph would reply that his god was worshipped at sacrificial altars, on hills where lilies and cyclamen grew without the help of man; then the child would answer that Joseph ought to see the tiny iris that came out of the desert when the crocodile called back the waters of the Nile.

The queen loved her gardens. The lakes, the artificial hills, and the flowers were pleasing to her. She also loved life, and we can picture her holding feasts and banquets in the garden, with Joseph standing behind her, keeping off the flies with a big ostrich fan. There were hunting parties and festivals on the water, intense brilliancy everywhere—the sun shone perpetually. In this atmosphere Amenophis IV. grew up, a quiet, studious boy, delighting in nature, walking in the garden, listening to the birds, smelling the flowers, following the butterflies. He was already married to Nefertiti, an Egyptian girl of great beauty.

One of his first acts as Pharaoh was the completion of a temple to Ra-Horakhti at Karnak. Carved in the cliff was a figure of the Pharaoh worshipping Amon. Above the figure the disk of the sun appears and from it stream long lines terminating in hands, a representation which afterwards became the symbol of a new interpretation of the old belief of the sun worship in Heliopolis. Originally the sun's disk was worshipped as Ra, or Amon, or Ra-Horakhti-Aton. Amenophis IV. conceived the god as the power which created the sun, the energy which penetrated to this earth and caused all things to grow.

Amon-Ra and the old gods of Egypt were for the most part but deified mortals. To Amenophis he was the father of mankind, made manifest in sunshine, to be sought among flowers and trees, the wild birds and the fishes.

As the first apostle of the simple life, he urged his people to worship in truth without excess of ritual.

No graven images were allowed.

The True God had no form.

The symbol of the religion was the sun's disk, with the rays ending in hands, but the symbol was not to be worshipped. God was a formless deity, a life-giving intangible essence. Sunrise and sunset were the hours for ceremonial adoration.

Amenophis IV. wrote very beautiful hymns. In one of them we find the following:

> "Thy rising is beautiful in the horizon of heaven, O Living Aton, who guidest all countries that may make laudations at thy dawning and at thy setting.
>
> "When the Aton rises all the land is in joy.
> His rays produce eyes for all he has created; and men say
> 'It is life to see Him,
> There is death in not seeing Him.'"

According to old beliefs the soul of a man had to pass through awful places up to the judgment throne of Osiris, where he was weighed in the balances. If he was found wanting, he was devoured by a ferocious monster, but if the scales turned in his favor he was accepted into the Elysian Fields.

Amenophis rejected this old belief of Osiris and his judgment throne. He believed that when a man died his soul continued to exist as an immaterial ghost, sometimes in the dreamy halls of heaven, and sometimes visiting, in shadowy form, the haunts of its earthly life.

Finding it impossible to develop his ideals and reforms in Thebes, he decided to build a new city, far away, where he could worship his god and hold his court free from all tiresome old conventions, away from the greed and hypocrisy of the priesthood which was exerting a contaminating influence against his reforms. He changes his name from Amenophis, "the peace of Amon," to Akhnaton, "Aton is satisfied."

Meanwhile what has become of Joseph? Sad to relate, unjustly he has been put in prison where the king's prisoners were bound. There he gained the good will of the keeper and was put in charge of other offenders of the Pharaoh. Joseph fortunately interpreted their dreams satisfactorily. Later he was brought before the Pharaoh to interpret for him his curious dreams of fat and lean kine, and again of the seven good ears of corn followed by the thin and blasted ones. Joseph interpreted them as the prophecy of seven plentiful years to be followed by seven years of famine.

The Pharaoh rewarded him by making him overseer of the agriculture of the country.*

Akhnaton starts out in the royal dahabiyah to choose a site for his new city and finds a perfect place between Heliopolis and Thebes where the limestone cliffs upon the east bank recede about three miles, returning to the river five or six miles further on, forming a bay with the river protecting it on the west side, and on all the other sides the cliffs, forming a crescent. In the river he saw a little island that he could use for pavilions and pleasure houses. Along the edge of the river he would place the villas for the nobles.

Beyond this verdant strip stretched the smooth desert where he might build his own palaces and great temples. Behind them the wilderness sloped up to the

---

*According to the latest authority Moses not Joseph may have been a contemporary of Akhnaton.

foot of the cliffs. Here he planned roads and causeways for chariot races, and in the cliffs he would cut his tomb and others for his followers. There would be along the river quays and palaces; their reflection in the river he could already imagine.

Before returning to Thebes he placed at intervals boundary stones as limits to the city. It took nine years of lavish expenditure and skill to transform these fields and wilderness into a city as fine as the world has ever seen. A noble, living there, describes it as "The Mighty City of the Horizon of Aton, great in loveliness, mistress of pleasant ceremonies, rich in possessions, the offering of the sun being in the midst. At the sight of her beauty there is rejoicing. She is lovely and beautiful; when one sees her it is like a glimpse of heaven." Arthur Weigall has given us a most wonderful picture of this extraordinary man whose conception of the deity far transcended any that had gone before. His hymns to Aton are very like various psalms familiar to us all.

His constant cry was "Oh Lord, how manifold are thy works!"

It was an idyllic life Akhnaton lived with Nefertiti in the garden city. No Egyptian woman ever had a freer life. She had her own chariot which she drove herself with her three little daughters. She went to festivals with Akhnaton. She is seen in the chariot with the Pharaoh's arm about her, her children in his lap, and he in the form and dress of a mere man. Pictures on the walls of the palace show her as very beautiful.

They drive through the streets of the High Priest and the King's Highway, which are lined with palaces and villas, set in the midst of gardens; granaries and storehouses stood near the white enclosing wall. They arrive at the "Precinct of Aton," a pleasure garden consisting of two large walled-in enclosures, the first of which was entered through a hall of thirty-six columns, beyond which there was a small fish pond covered with lotus flowers and lilies and enclosed in trees; at the side of the enclosure stood a house, a farm for cattle, sheep and ducks; in the second enclosure was a large lake on which pleasure boats floated. Stretching along on the north side a colonnade furnished a shady place for one to sit and watch the splendor of the sun reflected in the water. In a corner of the enclosure a little kiosk rose on columns sunk in tanks of water, filled with lotus flowers. Its wall and pillars were painted with clusters of purple grapes and red pomegranates, blue lotus flowers and green leaves, with wild ducks flying against the azure sky. A path flanked by flower beds led to another little lake with an island, approached by an ornamental bridge.*

In the midst of this idyllic life we will leave Akhnaton, the pacifist, who abhorred war, but loved to spend the profits of the wars carried on by his grandfather. He remained ever unmindful of his generals, who were striving to pay his soldiers in distant provinces of the realm.

By the time of Akhnaton, the Sumerian culture had reached its apex in the island of Crete. Its history runs parallel with the Egyptian and is delightfully told by Sir Arthur Evans. One wonders if the destruction or desertion of the beautiful palace of Knossus was due to Akhnaton's indifference and neglect of his sea-islands, of which Crete was the most important. There the palace of Knossus stood in a commanding position, built on the ruins of civilization upon civilization, where now in the twentieth century the magic spade of Sir Arthur Evans has dug out priceless treasures, which reveal to

---
*Life and Times of Akhnaton. Arthur Weigall. Courtesy of G. P. Putnam's Sons.

us moderns the height of civilization reached 2000 years before our Christian era began. The palace was practically a city combining temple and living quarters for a vast number of people. Built around a great court, open to the sky, galleries ran to all parts of the palace, which was really a city. The galleries twisted and turned and finally brought one to the temple where the dual divinities, the Mother Earth and the infant Zeus, were symbolized by the double ax, from which word in its Greek form Labrys, came our word labyrinth. This double ax symbol was used extensively in the decoration of the hall. Serpents and bulls were pictured in temple rites, but more interesting to garden lovers is the use of the rose, the iris and the lily decorating the women's quarters. A row of turquoise blue olive trees on a red background is most effective.

While the excavations of Sir Arthur Evans have not indicated any provision for a garden in the great palace enclosed with high walls and lighted by air shafts, one knows that the whole island was a natural garden, where in olive orchards the iris, the wild rose, the lily must have grown in profusion. The great industry of the island was olive oil, shipped to all parts of the world in huge jars made on the island. One was dug up at Tel-El-Amarna. In the gem of a salon in the Metropolitan Museum there is a reproduction of one of these decorated with a shaft of the field lily, so delicate it seems almost alive, and might have been picked in a New England field. Human figures are very alive, full of action, and dressed in brilliant colors, suggestive of later Persian art. The representation of wild life reminds one of the decoration in the palaces of Queen Tiy and Akhnaton, and tempts one to believe that Cretan artists were brought to Egypt by Thothmes III., the grandfather of Akhnaton.

About three hundred years after the days of Akhnaton, a group of pilgrims were on their way to the Feast of Dedication of the wonderful temple Solomon had just completed in Jerusalem. Wearied by their long march and jostled by the crowd bringing from the hills oxen and sheep for the sacrifice, they took refuge in a garden of olives. An eminent seer is telling the children the story of their ancestors in Egypt. How hard they had been forced to work in the gardens there, where ponds and fountains required great engineering skill. Trees were brought from distant lands and they had even made a garden for the Pharaoh to live in.

A boy asks why the Israelites ever went to Egypt. The seer then unfolded the history of the children of Israel and told the story of the Garden of Eden; how Jahve, their own God, created the heavens and the earth, and covered the land with trees and herbs and made the animals and placed them there; but there was no one to till the land or subdue the animals. So he made man in his own image, breathing into him the spirit of life, that he might make of the garden a pleasant place for Jahve to walk in, in the cool of the day.

The boy was thrilled as the seer went on to tell of the wonderful gardens he had seen as he passed through Media and Persia, a land of hills and forests, where trees were venerated, and the planting and care of them was a sacred occupation, and an important part in the education of a boy.

While the seer made very little mention of flowers, he did say that wherever they were cultivated they were enclosed with hedges, and were near the houses of the women's quarters.

Looking across the valley to the new temple on the hill the question arises, did Solomon have gardens around the palace? One who had worked there told how the palace was built on terraces leading up to the temple which was to be the home of the Ark. A great porch was lined with cedar wood and the roof was supported with columns, the capitals of which were fashioned like the lily. Here Solomon would judge his people. The great doors were carved with palm leaves and the walls covered with nets of checker work (we call it lattice). Long rows of pomegranates were carved out of wood and overlaid with gold. The description reminds one of the palace of Knossus, destroyed by earthquake centuries before. Gold was lavishly used and the cedar wood Hiram brought from Lebanon and far-away Spain. Below the porch a molten sea was fashioned like the flower of a lily, and this was to be for the use of the priests. All the sacrificial basins within the temple were also shaped like the lily.

While there is no mention of gardens in the account given in 1st Kings, ch. 6 and 7, the Song of Solomon leaves no doubt in our minds as to the beauty of the gardens though it is more suggestive of Arabia than Palestine, and very likely was taken from Sumerian and Babylonian sources, as were many of the Biblical and Grecian myths.

The "Song of Solomon" is of Spring and we read:

> "Lo the winter is passed—
>   The rain is over and gone
>   The Flowers appear on the earth
>   The time of the singing of birds is come
>   And the voice of the turtle-dove is heard in our land.
>   The fig ripeneth her green figs
>   The Vines are in blossom,
>   They give forth their fragrance.

* * *

> My beloved is gone down to his garden
> To the beds of spices
> To feed in the garden and to gather lilies
> He feedeth his flocks among the lilies.
>
> I went down into the garden of nuts
> To see the green plants of the valley
> To see whether the vine budded
> And the pomegranates were in flower."

When history fails to record facts imagination runs riot. I believe Biblical critics are still in doubt as to what period the Song of Solomon belongs. Imagination tempts us to attribute it to the Queen of Sheba, the story of whose visit to Solomon is so graphically told in the Book of Chronicles. Surely her visit was not only to satisfy her curiosity about the great king in the north. Undoubtedly she had a matrimonial project in mind and when she found Solomon well supplied with wives with the recent addition of the Egyptian princess to whom she would have to hold an inferior place, she gave up the project and returned to her gardens to dream of a simple life in the companionship of the wisest man she had ever met.

One would like to linger in these gardens gathering the lilies that Solomon in all his glory could not rival; or better still wander over the hills of Galilee where rocks shelter the cyclamen and anemones that Joseph loved, on through meadows gay as mosaic floors with a riot of wild flowers, down to the green pastures and the still waters from whence dreams and fancies take their flight.

CHAPTER II

AMONG THE GREEKS

"To rejoice in life, to find the world beautiful
and delightful to live in marked the Greek Spirit,
and distinguished it from all that had gone before."
The Greek Way—EDITH HAMILTON

CHAPTER II

LEAVING the Orientals for a while, we find a little country not far away, developing in a manner quite different from the Egyptian way. It was a land of sea and mountains, where natural barriers divided the isolated states, and required independence of life. Here a race of individualists developed, dependent on agriculture, to whom the contending with nature was a joy.

To the Greek all nature is personified. The sky is Zeus stretching over the land, lightning and cloud are his messengers. Water is very precious and must be protected from all pollution, therefore springs are guarded by nymphs. While in Egypt the Sun was the supreme God, in Greece Earth and Water are apparently more sacred. Myths develop; many are imported from Syria, and while Hiram was collecting cypresses in the west for the building of Solomon's temple, Homer is weaving the myths into poetry.

In the Odyssey we find a description of the garden of Alcinous, Nausicaa's father, which is the model for the homes of the well-to-do in the early days of the Greeks.

"From outside the court, by its entry, extends a great garden of four acres, fenced each way. In it flourish tall trees: pears or pomegranates, stone fruits gaudy with their ripening load, also sweet figs and heavy-bearing olives. The fruit of these trees never blights or fails to set, winter and summer, through all the years. A west wind blows there perpetually, maturing one crop and making another. Pear grows old upon pear, and apple upon apple, with bunch after bunch of grapes and fig after fig. Here, too, a fertile vineyard has been planted for the King. A part of this lies open to the sun, whose rays bake its grapes to raisins, while men gather ripe grapes from the next part and in a third part tread out the perfected vintage in wine-presses. On one side are baby grapes whose petals yet fall; on another the clusters empurple towards full growth. Beyond the last row of trees, well laid garden plots have been arranged, blooming all the year with flowers. And there are two springs, one led throughout the orchard ground, whilst the other dives beneath the sill of the great court to gush out beside the stately house: from it the citizens draw their water. Such were the noble gifts the gods had lavished upon the palace of Alcinous."*

Marie Luise Gothein, the great garden history authority, says that the "flowers in these well laid garden plots" were only vegetables, that at this period horticulture was not practised—but I cannot believe it! Possibly they were herbs in flower, but beets and spinach, never!

Greek mythology is full of the praise of flowers. Many charming legends tell of the transformation of divinities into plant or flower, bird or butterfly. Different flowers are the attributes of gods and goddesses. The rose and myrtle were sacred to Aphrodite, the laurel to Daphne, the olive to Pallas Athene, the poppy to Demeter, the vine to Dionysus. The celestials live above Olympus, and Zeus, tiring of their company, visits the homes of mortals. To reach the Earth he must pass the gate of clouds over which presides Demeter, pictured in the Iliad as the Goddess of the fields or the earth itself.

Like all myths, this one changed and grew. At first unwritten, it passed from mouth to mouth, the details changing, while underlying all remains the mystery of natural phenomena.

---

*Translated by T. E. Shaw (Lawrence of Arabia). Courtesy of the Oxford University Press, London.

One of Demeter's names means a gift. "She gave men the first fig in one place and in another the poppy. She is the mother of the vine; she knows the magic power of certain plants to bane or bless; she also presides over springs. At first she is the goddess of the fertility of the earth in its wildness but develops, as the goddess of agriculture, the fertility of the earth, when furthered by human skill. She taught the old Titans how to mow. She lays her finger on the earth and a new flower springs up. She haunts the fields in the spring and visits the barns in the autumn. She presides over the farm where the yearly labors become to the farmer acts of worship." In the Odyssey we find Persephone queen of the dead and in Hesiod the two are brought together.

Walter Pater, in his "Greek Studies" says that no chapter in the history of human imagination is more curious than the myth of Demeter and Persephone. The story preserved in the Homeric Hymns was long lost and finally found in 1780 in the manuscripts of the Imperial Library of Moscow. The hymn was probably written for one of the contests which took place on the seventh day of the Eleusian festival in which a bunch of ears of corn was the prize.

"I begin the song of Demeter," says the sacristan of the holy places, "the song of Demeter and her daughter Persephone whom Aidoneus carried away by the consent of Zeus, as she played apart from her mother with the deep-bosomed daughters of the Ocean, gathering flowers in a meadow of soft grass, roses and the crocus and fair violets and flags, and hyacinths and above all the strange flower of the narcissus,* which the earth, favoring the desire of Aidoneus brought forth for the first time to snare the footsteps of the flower-like girl.

---
*Asphodel.

A hundred heads of blossom grew up from the roots of it and the sky and the earth and the salt wave of the sea were glad at the scent thereof. She stretched forth her hand to take the flower; thereupon the earth opened and the king of the great nation of the dead sprung out with his immortal horses. He seized the unwilling girl, and bore her away weeping on his golden chariot. She uttered a shrill cry, calling upon her father Zeus; but neither man nor god heard her voice nor even the nymphs of the meadow where she played; except Hecate only, the daughter of Perseus sitting, as ever, in her cave, half veiled with a shining veil, thinking delicate thoughts; she and the sun also heard her."*

Demeter, overwhelmed with grief, searched the world to find her beloved child. At last she hears of her in the realm of Pluto, where with him she reigns queen of the dead. Zeus is petitioned to allow her to return to the world of light, but, alas, she has bitten a pomegranate given her by Pluto and only through compromise is allowed to return to the earth for a half of the year.

"As the religion of Demeter carries us back to the cornfields of Greece, and places us in fancy among a primitive race in the furrow and beside the granary, so the religion of Dionysus carries us back to its vineyards and is a monument of the ways and thoughts of people whose days go by beside the wine press." . . . In its earliest form Dionysus is "the soul of the individual vine, then the soul of the whole species, the spirit of fire and dew; alive and leaping in a thousand vines, he comes at last to have a scope equal to that of Demeter in a realm as wide and mysterious as hers. The whole productive power of the

---

*Homeric Hymn. Greek Studies. Walter Pater. Courtesy of Macmillan Co.

earth is in him. He journeys through the earth bearing gifts to every people."*

The legend of his birth tells us that his mother was a mortal. Giving birth to her son in seven months she dies by fire. The father, Zeus, takes the motherless child and nourishes him in his thigh. Zeus being the sky, his thigh becomes the lower cloud which brings the rain. From the lightning which killed his mother, the child was protected by the cooling cloud of the sky, and became the symbol of all tender things which grow out of a hard soil, as come the flowers of the spring.

His first name, Dithyrambus, signifies his two births, fire and dew, and was later given to the choral singing of his worshippers, music wild and boisterous as might be expected from the primitive people of Boetia.

The study of Greek mythology shows the enormous part played by village ritual and custom in forming the great legends. The aboriginal peasants of Greece sang and danced about their field magic, their fertility cycles and their year daemons from the earliest antiquity. Then came the migrations with their stirring events. Instead of crops people talked of heroes and their great deeds and the Epic Lays that arose were undoubtedly full of historic persons and events, losing their identity in the personification of mythical characters. Under the spell of these myths the Athenians developed.

Meanwhile the Spartan, Lycurgus, travelled about the world to find out what made nations great. He brought home a code of laws under the enforcement of which the Spartans developed into the strongest people of Greece through the glorification of the body. The Athenians on the other hand loved beauty rather than war and cultivated the mind in addition to the body.

*Greek Studies. Walter Pater. Courtesy of Macmillan Co.

In the year 776 B. C., the first Olympiad was held, in which the rival cities contended for supremacy.

Lycurgus also brought back the story of the city King Sargon founded above Nineveh surrounding it with a great wall, within which on an artificial hill, he built his palace and planted his garden with flowers and herbs brought from the land of the Hittites and the hills called Amanus. He told how Sargon's son Sennacherib built his palace also on artificial terraces which he said had no equal, and in his water system he took great pride, bringing from a distant hill water to fill his pond in which he planted diverse kinds of reeds for use in his house.

In less than a hundred years these palaces were destroyed by Nebuchadnezzar, king of Babylon, who, not wishing to be outdone by the Persians, built himself a still more lordly city covering a square equal in area to London and New York put together. (?) He surrounded it with a wall fifty times as high as a man and broad enough for a chariot to drive on. In the wall were one hundred huge brass gates through which the river Euphrates flowed across the city. To please his wife Amyites, a maiden from Media, the land of hills and terraces, he built his palace and the famous Hanging Gardens of Babylon in 700 B. C.

"The celebrated gardens, covering a square four hundred feet on every side, were carried up in terraces one above the other until they were as high as the walls of the city; from terrace to terrace were stairs ten feet wide. The terraces were built over arches, one above the other, and strengthened by a wall twenty-two feet thick. On top of the arches were first laid large flat stones sixteen feet long and four feet broad. Over these was a layer of reeds mixed with quantities of bitumen upon which were laid two rows of brick closely cemented together. The whole was covered with thick sheets of lead upon which lay the mould of the garden and all this floorage was contrived to keep the moisture of the mould from running away through the arches. The earth laid thereon was so deep that large trees might take root in it, and with such the terraces were covered as well as with all other plants and flowers that were proper to adorn a pleasure garden. In the upper terrace there was an engine by which water was drawn up out of the river and from whence the whole garden was watered. In the spaces between the several arches upon which this whole structure rested were large and magnificent apartments, that were very light and had the advantage of a beautiful prospect."*

The prosperity of Greece tempted Cyrus to annex it to his vast empire. He had already conquered Lydia and acquired the wealth of Croesus. Then Babylon was added and by the end of the seventh century all that remained was "Little Greece." Against Darius and Xerxes, "Little Greece" drove the Persians out of the country. Nor was this accomplished so much by the power of arms, as by the cleverness of mind of the great patriots then in power: Pisistratus, Themistocles, and Aristides.

During the time of Pisistratus the Homeric stories were put into literary form and written. This gave a new impetus to the intellectual life then awakening in Greece, and one hot day in August a real little boy was working in his father's vineyard up in the hills above Eleusis. He often stopped to rest under the vines which gave a pleasing shelter from the scorching sun. He had much to think about. In April he had taken part for the first time in his life in the chorus of boys who, singing

---
*Herodotus.

dithyrambs, escorted the old wooden image of Dionysus from the Lenaeum to the temple in the neighborhood of the Acropolis and back again. This was the year when the little god had been awakened from his winter's sleep up in the distant mountains of Boetia. The boy had heard how the priestesses, singing and dancing, had assembled at the shrine on the shortest day of the year and taken the god from his cradle.

In April he had taken part in the festival celebrating the mystical resurrection of Dionysus. Now it was August and during these months he had thought and wondered a great deal concerning these things. Suddenly there appeared before him a beautiful youth, languidly leaning against the vine, pouring from a bowl in his hand, wine on the ground. From his shoulder had fallen a wild goat skin and on his head rested an ivy crown. He was a stranger, and the boy, having grown up in the atmosphere of hospitality, offered him food and wine. The youth yawned and stretching himself said, "Wine! I am weary of wine, for months I have been feasted and feted through the length and breadth of the land. Wine and Mirth? I am tired of both, would that it were my lot to work in the vineyards as you do, Aeschylus; I am Dionysus, God of the vine, and must visit the vineyards of the world. Let it be your work to write the stories of the Gods which may inspire in your countrymen noble thoughts and noble deeds."

Through a dream came the inspiration to Aeschylus to devote his life to the writing of Greek tragedy, and Dionysus became not only the god of wine but of poetic inspiration. In later days he often was confused with Apollo and Orpheus.

After the defeat of the Persians in 480 B. C., the Golden Age of Greece dawned. Athens rose again from its ashes to be rebuilt by Pericles and adorned by Phidias. Theatres were built on the hillsides and great dramas, retelling the well-known stories of the myths, were acted in the open air on stages with backgrounds of marvelous beauty.

Aeschylus put new meaning into the myths. Though he watched the building of the Parthenon, he did not live to see it completed.

Herodotus wrote his history of the Persian wars and to him we owe the description of the Hanging Gardens of Babylon.

Reports from the East told of the rose gardens of Midas and Darius, magnificent parks of such size and beauty they were supposed to have been founded by the mythical queen Semiramis. Word comes to Greece that the Persian king is zealously cared for so that he may find gardens wherever he goes, and they are called Paradise and are full of all things fair and good that the earth can bring forth. Travelers speak of the prettiness of it all and the sweet odours which follow their steps.

The Golden Age lasted only fifty years. Then the rivalry of Athens and Sparta developed into the Peloponnesian War which lasted twenty-seven years, during which time the country people were, many of them, obliged to abandon their farms and take refuge in the city of Athens where there was no room for gardens. For the festival of Adonis, which came in August, the women planted quick-growing seeds in earthen pots. The seeds shot up quickly and died in a few days, symbolic of the short life of Adonis, the god of fertility. These pots were placed, with an image of the god, on the flat roofs of the houses and led to the permanent decoration of the roofs, transforming them into gardens of potted plants, which were known everywhere, as Adonis Gardens.

A Greek friend tells me that many Greek women still make these Adonis gardens, especially those living in the vicinity of Athens and its suburbs. They have apparently forgotten the symbolism of the gardens, but yearly plant the seeds in little jars or pots. Some of them think the offering must be in honor of the Panagia, the Greek Virgin; again transferring a cherished pagan custom to Christian observance.

In contrast to the Oriental garden as a pleasure ground for the despotic ruler, the Greeks used their gardens for the benefit of the state. The democratic conditions that deprived the private citizen of the means to maintain gardens on a large scale, proved favorable for the development of the public parks. At first these were simply groves about the temples, where public games were held in honor of a god. They grew into centers for social intercourse, where the citizens could walk on well-kept walks, or sit by cool springs under the shade of lofty trees.

Private gymnasiums and baths followed and developed into Academies which served as settings for symposiums and classes. Plato found the public places too noisy and crowded for his purpose and moved his school into his own garden, which he finally gave to the school; the school lasting until the time of Justinian in the sixth century A. D. Apparently the garden included several buildings where Plato and other leaders lived. Often the students made for themselves little huts or arbours where they too could live close to the school. Other philosophers had similar schools, or academies, as they were called.

By this time Alexander had led the Greeks into Asia where all its elaborate garden culture showed Oriental wealth and splendor. As democracy had restricted the ownership and development of private estates, many of the country gentlemen moved to Asia, Africa and Sicily. Egypt then became easily accessible, contributing a new splendor to the parks and gardens. Flowers were grown all the year round and used in great profusion to decorate the halls at the time of festivals. The Greeks brought into the new Hellenic cities the idea of public gardens which, joining royal estates, occupied a large proportion of the city area.

The city of Alexandria was built at this time and rivaled Athens as a center of learning. The city was laid out and built in Oriental splendor, but Antioch surpassed it in the beauty of its gardens. Marie Luise Gothein says that:

"The town (Antioch) had a wonderful site. The main street was a long continuous portico, with houses on one side, and on the other side gardens extending right to the foot of the mountains, with all manner of summer houses, baths and fountains, laid out in regular form."*

A suburb called Daphne was famed as the fairest spot on earth, with its porticoes, baths and fountains and sweet smelling aromatic odors. At the death of Alexander, his kingdom was divided among his officers, one of whom became Ptolemy I., to whom was given Egypt.

While the poetic fire of Greece was quenched by all its troubles, the spark blazed up again in Sicily, where Theocritus immortalized the peasant life in his charming idylls. Andrew Lang says that he "did more than borrow a note from the country people. He brought the gifts of his own spirit to the contemplation of the world. He had the clearest vision and the most ardent love of poetry." "Not of wars nor of tears, but of Pan would

---

*History of Garden Art, Vol. I, p. 73. Marie Luise Gothein. Courtesy of E. P. Dutton & Co.

he chant and of the neat-herds he sweetly sang, and singing he shepherded his flocks." This was the training Sicily, her hills, her seas, her lovers, her poet shepherds gave to Theocritus.

The old Dorian settlers pleased themselves with the fable that their fountain, Arethusa, had once been a Grecian nymph who, like themselves, had crossed the sea to Sicily. Many other myths and legends came from Greece to Sicily and took deep root there. Enna is supposed to be the site of the kidnapping of Persephone. In the centuries between the writing of the Homeric Hymns and the time of Theocritus the episode of Demophoon had changed into the story of Triptolemus, where we find Demeter, while searching for Persephone, resting, weary and tired, before the home of a peasant who, returning from his work, takes pity upon her and brings her into his humble dwelling where his only son is tossing in the fever of some dread disease. Demeter, moved with compassion, mixes some poppy seeds in water and gives the concoction to the child, who immediately falls into a blessed sleep. When all is quiet in the household, Demeter takes the child in her arms and is about to lay him on the burning embers, when the mother springs forward and snatches the child from the goddess, who then reveals herself and tells the mother that though she has prevented her wish to make the child immortal, she will some day return and make him wise and useful. After many years she comes again and teaches Triptolemus to plow, and in her chariot, drawn by dragon flies, she carries him over the earth, scattering seeds as they go.

Among the seeds there surely must have been rosemary which still grows in such profusion over the island. The hillsides in April are exquisite with its long branches of sage green foliage and blue clusters, and the air is sweet with its fragrance. Asphodel must have been there too, for all the wild places along the roadsides are covered with this decorative plant, called by the ancients Narcissus. It is associated with Persephone, as the story mentions that she had it in her hand when Pluto snatched her out of the garden, and to this day it is associated with death. People will not pick it or have it in the house because it is supposed to bring death in its train.

While Theocritus so dearly loved the country he has also left an extraordinarily vivid picture of the city of Alexandria; founded not very long before, it had taken the place of Athens as the center of intellectual life, though keeping many Oriental characteristics. An account of the coronation feast of Ptolemy Philadelphus gives us a clear idea of the opulence and luxury of the life.

"The inner pavilion in which the guests reclined contained one hundred and thirty-five couches. The awnings over the roof were vividly embroidered; arcades were draped with the skins of animals and purple tissues. One open to the air, was shady with the foliage of myrtles and laurels. Everywhere the ground was carpeted with flowers (though the season was midwinter), with roses, and white lilies and blossoms of the gardens. Gorgeous processions followed and finally a mask of the seasons swept by, Dionysus himself coming along in a chariot, a gigantic figure, clad in purple, pouring libations out of a golden cup."*

Nothing could be a greater contrast to this Oriental feast than the picture in Idyll VII where, at the farm of Phrasidemus, "we reclined on deep beds of fragrant lentils, lowly strewn, and rejoicing we lay in new stripped leaves of the vine. And high above our heads waved many a poplar, many an elm tree, while close at hand the sacred water from the nymph's own cave welled forth with murmurs musical. On the shadowy boughs the

---
*Andrew Lang. Preface to Theocritus and His Age, p. xxxi. Golden Treasury Series. Courtesy of Macmillan Co.

burnt cicadas kept their chattering call, far off the little owl cried in the thick thorn brake, the larks and finches were singing, the ring-dove moaned, the yellow bees were flitting about the springs. All breathed the scent of opulent summer, of the season of fruits: pears at our feet, apples by our sides were rolling plentiful, the tender branches with wild plums laden were earthward bowed, and the four year old pitch seal was loosened from the mouth of the wine jars. Ye nymphs of Castaly that hold the steep of Parnassus, say, was it ever a bowl like this that old Chiron set before Heracles in the rocky cave of Pholas? Was it nectar like this that beguiled the shepherd to dance and foot it about his folds, the shepherd that dwelt by Anapus, once on a time, the strong Polyphemus, who hurled at ships with mountains? Had these ever such a draft as ye nymphs bade flow for us by the altar of Demeter of the threshing floor? Ah, once again may I plant the great fan on her corn-heap, while she stands smiling by, with sheaves and poppies in her hands."*

And now if you happen to be on the slopes of Parnassus on May Day, you may take part in a charming festival where children go through the country with wreaths on their heads, and on the doors of their homes hang garlands of flowers all in honor of the ancient festival commemorating the return of Persephone to the land of light, bringing spring to the world. The yearly festival, celebrated on the third of June, with pagan pomp and splendor, in the vale of Enna, in honor of the Madonna is undoubtedly a direct descendant of Persephone's festival and in our Easter festival we surely see its survival.

---

*Idylls of Theocritus. Translation by Andrew Lang. Courtesy of Macmillan Co.

The same Greek friend who told me about the survival of the Adonis gardens tells me that if one goes into a Greek home practically anywhere in the world, he is sure to find there a pot of basil, or perhaps several. It is regarded as a blessed plant, which brings an atmosphere of health and purity into the house. With the Greek instinct to combine the aesthetic and the practical, the herb is used for flavoring meats and salads, and it adorns the sunniest window in the house.

It is claimed that many of the early myths that form the backbone of Grecian literature originated in the ancient civilization of Crete, where the earliest deity was the earth mother symbolized by the serpent whose writhings caused the frequent and devastating earthquakes to which the island was subject. A much later representation is seen on an ivory, where the goddess is seated on a throne with the infant Zeus on her knee, his little hands out-stretched to the world.

CHAPTER III

AMONG THE ROMANS

The word by seers and sibyls told,
In groves of oak, or fanes of gold
Still floats upon the morning wind,
Still whispers to the willing mind.

EMERSON

CHAPTER III

SPRING dawns again! Persephone brings back her flowers, the almond trees are white with blossoms; asphodel and rosemary cover the hills of Sicily. The earth rejoices and over all reigns the sun.

Around the point a little boat enters the bay of Syracuse. The nymph in the fountain of Arethusa splashes her welcome as a student from Athens springs ashore, and curls himself up by her side, while Pan sitting nearby pipes him a tune. The student is Quintus Horatius Flaccus, commonly known as Horace. He was being educated in one of the academies, when the news of Caesar's assassination reached Greece. Brutus came through, fighting Caesar's friends, calling Caesar a tyrant, opposed to Liberty, and Horace with other students enlisted in Brutus' army. He fought at Philippi against young Octavius Caesar and Mark Antony, until Brutus was beaten and fell on his sword. Horace fled and Octavius was soon busy parcelling out the estates of his enemies among those who had fought for him, Horace's nice little patrimony among them. Octavius was also studying in Athens at the time of the uprising and may have known and liked Horace. At any rate he pardoned him and allowed him to return to Rome, a penniless clerk.

The Rome he returned to had become completely Hellenized and the Romans found the "Greek Way" most attractive in the manner of villas and gardens. Many of them had been developed in Hellenistic days, and now belonged to Roman gentlemen whose wealth allowed them the luxury of at least two residences and often more.

Maecenas had a very large estate on the Esquiline and much wealth. He loved feasts and company. Virgil introduces Horace to him and he finds him most interesting, especially when his ready wit and polished humor tossed him a well turned verse, showing up the vanities and failures of the men about him. Sometimes it hurt, but it put new life into men; the crowd admired the beauty and gaiety of his verses, all of which added to the popularity of Maecenas.

According to Dr. McGiffert:

"The prevailing culture of the world was Hellenic; from the time of Alexander's conquest, Greek influence had been transforming the civilization of Egypt and western Asia. And when the Hellenized East became a part of Rome's dominion the same influences made themselves felt in the west. The Greeks lacked the genius for government, but possessed the power of impressing themselves, their culture, their ideas, their beliefs, upon other peoples to a degree shared by no other race."[*]

The Roman builders copied the Greeks and built their villas around an open court; they chose sites of great beauty, they used an ordered, regular plan, connecting house and garden with colonnade or pergola leading to a Nymphaeum where it was possible to escape the burning sun of a Roman summer.

A striking feature about Roman property is the way in which a man's belongings were scattered about. Cicero, in addition to what he inherited bought in his lifetime seventeen other estates. In some cases these were united or connected to each other to give him varied bits of scenery; a glimpse of a snow capped peak; a flash of the blue sea; rolling hills or verdant pasture. Again,

---
[*]A. C. McGiffert, Apostolic Age. Courtesy of Charles Scribner's Sons.

lands were added that he might find the right soil and exposure for different crops. The hills were covered with vineyards and olive orchards, introduced from Greece. As guests of Cicero in his Tusculan villa, we linger in the peristyle, discussing with statesmen the topics of the day; the need of agricultural reform, and the impossibility of working the farm without slave labor; we listen to the philosophers discussing the decline of the old Latin stock, or the danger of bringing the Oriental cults into rivalry with Roman gods. Looking up the long path leading to the Nymphaeum we see Horace and Virgil and quickly join them in Horace's favorite pergola from which we watch the late afternoon shadows fall on the Campagna stretching away in the distance to the little city of Rome. Horace is in fine humor and recites to us his newly composed "Ode in Praise of Country Life":

> "Happy the man, who far from town's affairs,
> The life of old world mortals shares;
> With his own oxen tills his forbears' fields,
> Nor thinks of usury and its yields—
> No soldier he, by the fierce bugle called,
> Nor sailor at each storm appalled;
> He shuns the forum and the haughty gate
> Of nobles stronger than the state.
> His business is, round poplars tall, to twine
> The ripe young layers of the vine;
> Or in some quiet valley to survey
> His lowing heifers as they stray.
> Now with his knife the worthless shoots he lops
> Grafting instead for richer crops;
> Draws the new honey, in pure jars to keep,
> Or shears the timid staggering sheep.
> When Autumn, with his mellow fruitage gay,
> Doth o'er the fields his head display,
> What joy it is the grafted pears to try,
> And grapes which with sea-purple vie;

* * *

> What joy beneath some palm-oak old and gray
> Or on thick turf our limbs to lay;
> While streams past toppling banks roll down their flood,
> And the birds croon in every wood,
> And fountains murmur with their gushing streams
> Sounds that shall soothe to sleep and dreams."

We laugh at Horace and tell him he never really could care so much for country life. "Suppose Maecenas calls for you tonight, will you refuse him?" He smiles and draws from his toga another poem as answer to our question. "Here, my friends, Hear what my valet has to say," and reads the delightful lines translated by the authors of the "Winged Horse" from which I have not received permission to quote but advise everyone to read—page 61.

Horace then goes on to tell us of his estate in the Sabine Hills, which Maecenas has just given him. He tells us that there is a range of hills broken only by a shady valley with the rising sun shining on its right slope, and the setting sun warming its left. The climate is most delightful and there is a spring which gives abundant water good for head troubles and stomach troubles too.

The first poems Virgil wrote were similar to those of Theocritus, and became very popular in Rome. They are charming pictures of farmers and shepherds, and country life in Italy, especially in the spring time, and captivate us as they did Maecenas, who gave him a villa in his own gardens on the Esquiline. The afternoon we met him at Cicero's villa he was absorbed in the composition of the Aeneid and recited to us certain passages in praise of trees. Again I would like to quote from the "Winged Horse," especially the summing up of the Georgics—delightful poems of farm life which every farmer today would find profitable, especially the one on bees.

Virgil died in 19 B. C. Ten years later Maecenas and Horace followed. Maecenas left his vast estate on the Esquiline to Augustus Caesar, who had made himself emperor. His boast is that he found Rome brick and left it marble. From this time the little city of Rome was called the "Eternal City." How beautiful it must have been with its chain of villas inside and outside the old walls.

While Augustus was building his great palace on the Palatine, he may have lived in a little house tucked away in the hills, or perhaps it belonged to Tiberius Claudius Nero, where his wife Livia allowed Augustus to make love to her, and finally persuade her to divorce Tiberius and marry him. Whatever the history of the house, it stands today to show us how charming a dwelling house could be in old Rome. There is a subterranean room frescoed to simulate a garden full of sweet-scented flowers, with a wooden fence, a broad path with a background of high trees and shrubs with birds on the branches, and a charming group of orange trees in bloom. There is also a rumor that it was in this room that Augustus received Virgil when he came to plead for the restoration of his father's farm.

Many of the Romans had villas in Pompeii where they went for sea breezes when Rome became unbearably hot. From the frescoes in these houses we learn much about garden art. They show the peristyle made into a garden, with beds around the walls filled with growing plants in the midst of which were little animals of marble, and statues of Hermes. In one there is a basin of water overflowing into another basin from which it descends over a little stairway into a round pond, as in later days the Renaissance architects made their famous water stairways. These frescoes also show us how highly developed the art of painting was in those days. We see beautiful coloring, colors that cannot be perfectly reproduced today, if they ever were, even in China. Perspective is well developed and the human figure is superb, and strong, or light and airy as the theme demands.

About fifty years after Augustus we have the picture of Nero watching the burning of Rome. On the ashes he built his famous Golden House. For this purpose he commissioned as architects, Severus and Celer, setting aside in the very heart of Rome a square mile and including the tops and slopes of three of Rome's seven hills. The whole space, so they say, was enclosed by three colonnades with a grand entrance portico on the side towards the forum. Within the enclosure, besides the imperial palace there were parks, gardens and vineyards; and extensive Thermae supplied not only with aqueduct water but with water from renowned sulphur springs, twelve miles distant; also sea water from the Mediterranean, and an immense lake, for naval sham fights, fed by torrents of water falling in cascades from the great reservoir on the Caelian. A colossal statue of Nero stood by the lake which later became the Colosseum.

Pliny the Elder saw the building of Nero's Golden House. He travelled a great deal. He knew the East and was familiar with the Adonis gardens. He went to Spain and Africa to study plant life and wrote a book about it, but when he returned to Rome and saw the imperial villas, he remarked, "Large estates have ruined Italy." He did not at all approve of Cicero's Tusculum villa which he considered too luxurious, though he admitted that it was in the spirit of the Greek Academy and that there one did meet the great men of Rome.

It is in the letters of Pliny the Younger to his friends Tacitus, Suetonius, and Trajan that we learn much of the life of a cultured Roman gentleman living in the first century A. D. In the description of his villa in Tuscany he mentions the beauty of the site overlooking the valley of the Arno. He lays special stress on the gardens which are in three groups.

1. The facade that is accessible from the front.
2. A group of buildings high up on the hill.
3. The hippodrome, the park, which is on one side of the house and adjoins the wing of the chief facade.

From the front can be seen a wide colonnade with two wings which contain the dining room and the living room. In the colonnade there is a little court planted with plane trees with a fountain in the center. Round the court are three rooms, one of which is described as a charming garden room with marble floor and walls painted with trees and birds in the branches. In front of the facade is the ornamental garden or what the Greeks called a xystus, where there is a lawn with flower beds edged with box. This is on the highest terrace and leading down to the next is more plantation with raised box borders clipped into various shapes of animals.

Pliny writes:

"In front of these agreeable buildings lies a very spacious hippodrome, entirely open in the middle, by which means the eye, upon the first entrance, takes in its whole extent at one view. It is encompassed on every side with plane trees covered with ivy so that while their heads flourish with their own green, their bodies enjoy a borrowed verdure; and the ivy, twining round the trunk and branches, spreads from tree to tree and links them together. Between the plane trees are planted box trees, and behind these laurels which blend their shade with that of the planes. The raised path around the hippodrome, which here runs straight, bends at the farther end into a semicircle and takes on a new aspect, being embowered in cypress trees and obscured by their denser and more gloomy shade; while the inner circular alleys (for there are several) enjoy the full sun. Further on there are roses too along the path; and the cool shade is pleasantly alternated with sunshine.

"Having passed through these manifold winding alleys the path resumes a straight course, and at the same time divides into several tracks, separated by box hedges. In one place you have a little meadow, in another the box is interspersed in groups, and cut into a thousand different forms; sometimes into letters expressing the name of the master, or again that of the artificer, whilst here and there little obelisks rise intermixed alternately with apple trees; when on a sudden, in the midst of this elegant regularity, you are surprised with an imitation of the negligent beauties of rural nature; in the center of which lies a spot surrounded with a knot of |dwarf plane trees. Beyond these are interspersed clumps of the smooth and twining acanthus; then comes a variety of figures and names cut in box.

"At the upper end is a semi-circular bench of white marble, shaded with a vine which is trained upon four pillars of carystian marble. Water gushing through several pipes under the bench falls into a stone cistern underneath from which it is received into a fine marble basin so artfully contrived that it is always full without ever overflowing. When I sup here, the tray of whets and the larger dishes are placed round the margin, while the smaller ones swim about in the farm of little ships and water fowl—opposite this is a fountain which is incessantly emptying and filling, for the water which it throws up to a great height falling back into it, is, by means of connected openings, returned as fast as it is received.

"Fronting the bench stands a chamber of lustrous marble whose doors project and open upon a lawn; from its upper and lower windows the eye ranges upward and downward over other spaces of verdure. In different quarters are disposed several marble seats, which serve as so many reliefs after one is wearied with walking. Next each seat is a little fountain; and throughout the whole hippodrome small rills conveyed through pipes run murmuring along, wheresoever the hand of art has seen proper to conduct them; watering here and there different spots of verdure, and in their progress bathing the whole."

While Pliny only caught a glimpse of the possibility that "nature unadorned" might add to the charm and interest of a garden, Tacitus, his friend, records in his annals that Nero availed himself "of the ruins of his country and built a house in which gems and gold were not so much to be admired as fields and lakes; and, as in deserts, here in woods; there, open spaces and prospects. The masters and designers being Severus and Celer, they had the genius and courage to attempt by art even what nature had denied."

Pliny's letter gives the best picture we have of the Roman classic garden. He had also a villa on Lake Como of which he writes most affectionately:

"How stands Como, the favorite scene of yours and mine? What becomes of the pleasant villa, the ever vernal portico, the shady plane tree grove, the crystal canal so agreeably winding along its flowery banks, together with the charming lake below, that serves at once the purpose of use and beauty? What have you to tell of the firm but springy avenue, the path exposed on all sides to full sunshine, the public salon, the private dining room, and all the elegant apartments for repose both at noon or night? Leave, my friend, the low and sordid pursuits of life to others, and in this safe and snug retreat, emancipate yourself for your studies."*

Hadrian's villa was a good example of an imperial villa, but it is hard to get much idea of it beyond that of size. In imperial times the suburban villas became more extended and magnificent while the houses inside the town were contracted and narrow, and it was most difficult to obtain any land for gardens. Window boxes then became common and roof gardens and balconies added to the pleasure of life.

In the provinces, the country houses and gardens included parks for hunting, and the villa habit extended through Gaul even into Britain but all these gardens perished in the years of war and turmoil in which the Roman Empire broke up.

---

*History of Garden Art: Marie Luise Gothein. Courtesy of E. P. Putnam Co.

CHAPTER IV

A PATH TO THE CLOISTER

"The artistic side of man insists upon the need of understanding and appreciating all good and desirable things. The ascetic side insists on the need of a power to resist them lest they should hinder the attainment of something better."

GILBERT MURRAY

CHAPTER IV

THE Mediterranean Sea was the great highway of Imperial Rome. From its ports roads led to the remotest limits of the Empire, and the Emperor's boast was that Rome had no frontiers. People of every race and creed travelled by land and sea and all that could sought Rome. Many brought new religions, for Rome was tolerant; Egyptians, Asiatics, and Greeks were allowed temples for their own cults.

In a grove on a promontory high above the bay of Naples stood a temple to Apollo; behind it, enhancing its beauty, stretched the blue sea. An underground passage descended from it to a cavern where dwelt the Cumean Sibyl, supposed to have foretold the coming of Christ. Nearby lay the Lake of Avernus where the Sibyl met Aeneas and directed him how to find the golden bough which should be his passport to Persephone.

From the Greek colony on the Bay of Naples ran the via Appia, the most important highway in ancient times, and led to Rome. On it travelled rich and poor. Hebrew merchants in chariots brought their wares to the Roman market, for there could be found whatever was to be had in the markets of the East. Some travelled by horse or mule with frequent relays, while others walked the weary way, some in chains, prisoners from conquered Syria. With these came Paul who was accused of sedition and had, as a Roman citizen, appealed to be tried in Rome. We hear nothing of his physical fatigue; his new religion gave him courage to believe that all his trials of shipwreck, hunger and the sword, were fitting him to preach the gospel of Jesus Christ to Jew and Gentile. We may picture him encouraging his fellow travellers, urging those who were already Christians to stand fast in the faith and to quit themselves like men.

It seems strange that Paul makes no mention of the beauty of the world in his journeys. He must have seen many a flower blooming in the gardens of Antioch and Athens but the only garden that interested him was the one filled with human plants to be trained and cultivated for the Kingdom of Heaven. He regarded each individual as a temple of God in which dwelt his spirit. Of his gardens he says that "one plants, another waters, but God gives the increase." We imagine it enclosed with the bond of fellowship while from the Holy Spirit wafts the fragrance of righteousness.

Though Paul gives us no description of Rome, Pater tells us that when Marius visited it in the second century A. D., his first visit was to the Palatine. Going through the Forum he stopped at the flower market and bought a zinnia to deck the folds of his toga. "Immediately before him on the steep height, where little old Rome had huddled itself together, arose the Palace of the Caesars. Half veiling it, the trim old-fashioned garden-walks, under their closely woven walls of dark and glossy foliage—test of long and careful cultivation—wound gradually among choice trees, statues and fountains, distinct and sparkling in the full morning sunlight, the richly tinted mass of pavilions and corridors above, centering in the lofty white marble dwelling place of Apollo himself."*

Pater speaks of the roses, lustrously yellow and red, coming during the winter from Carthage, and of how flowers were laid before the images of the gods in supplication for deliverance from the plague. Marius, the Epicurean, visited the Tusculum where he passed the haunted ruins of Cicero's villa on the wooded heights,

---

*Marius, the Epicurean. Walter Pater. Courtesy of the Macmillan Co.

and saw how the "numerous cascades of the precipitous garden, framed in the doorway of the hall, fell into a picture in which the power of the water was pleasant." Another day he goes to an old flower garden in the rear of the home of the Cicili. Here and there was set a venerable olive tree, "a picture in pensive shade and fiery blossom." Towards the west the garden was bounded by a low, grass-grown hill with an opening cut in the steep side which led into a crypt, originally a family sepulchre, now growing to be a vast Christian necropolis. The venerable beauty of the house and its precincts above were maintained here. Incense, lights, and flowers were disposed around for the worship or commemoration of the departed. The Christian Era had begun; the blending of Pagan customs with Christian.*

Baring Gould gives an interesting example of this on an old mosaic from an ancient palace near Pau. The pavement in the most important room of the palace "was bordered by an exquisite running pattern of vines and bunches of grapes springing from four drinking vessels in the centers of the north, south, east and west sides. The pattern within the border was of circles containing conventional roses, alternated folded and expanded"—in the midst of which appeared a great cross where as the arms intersected in the center there was a gigantic bust of Neptune with his trident. The four arms were filled with fish and other sea life. The Curé who apparently was with Baring Gould claimed it as a Christian symbol, though Baring Gould himself considered it a pagan god in a pagan house. Lying at the head of a pool it suggested an early Christian baptistry.

Similar mosaics are seen in the Ravenna churches, where pagan river gods surround the Good Shepherd.

---
*Curious Myths of the Middle Ages. S. Baring Gould. Courtesy Longmans Green & Co.

With the dawn of the Christian era church legends take the place of myths. In rural districts many of the old pagan festivals survive in the celebration of Saints' Days. Statues of Demeter and Dionysus are used as models for the Holy Mother and Child and possibly the old statues themselves are used. In the temple of Cnidus there was a statue of Demeter seated on the stone of sorrow and grieving for her child; this is regarded by some as the model for the "sorrowing Mother" of the Christian Church.

In the early days of Christianity, the women were usually the first to be converted. Saint Sabina, a Roman noblewoman, was converted by her slave Seraphina, and together they suffered martyrdom. Over her house one of the loveliest churches in Rome was built and named for her. Its gardens and vineyards are still used for monastic purposes. Saint Cecilia, another Roman noblewoman living in the third century, was brought up in the Christian faith but obliged to marry a pagan. Fortunately she converted him and all her household. According to legend she had an extraordinary talent for music and invented the organ, and wrote such beautiful hymns and sang them so sweetly that angels came from heaven to hear them. Her husband, returning from his baptism, saw one in her room, placing crowns of roses on both their heads. Alas! The whole household suffered martyrdom, but Pope Urban made her house a place of worship and remains of it can still be seen under the church erected in her honor.

In the fourth century Saint Helena, possibly the daughter of a British king and certainly the mother of the Emperor Constantine, discovered in the garden of Calvary the Cross on which Jesus was crucified. Saint Helena divided the cross in halves, one of which was left in Jerusalem; the other she carried to Constantinople. Part of this was sent to Rome where the Church of Santa Croce now guards it.

Her son, the Emperor Constantine, was much impressed by the Christian religion. Before an important battle he had a vision of a flaming cross in the sky with these words, "In hoc vinces." When the battle was about to begin he ordered his soldiers to carry the cross on to the field. The victory was his and he embraced Christianity and ordered his court to do the same.

From this time all but one of the Roman Emperors were Christian, at least in name. It is said that Constantine laid in Rome the foundations of a number of churches, among them the old Saint Peter's on the site of St. Peter's crucifixion.

For various reasons he moved his court to Byzantium where he built for himself a palace with terraced gardens ascending from the sea. We can only imagine the beauty of it from descriptions of later villas, for all trace of it has vanished. Undoubtedly it was eastern in plan and decoration like Hadrian's villa in Rome. As Constantine is supposed to have placed at St. Peter's the famous pineapple fountain court, we may imagine its mate in his garden at Constantinople.

In Constantinople, the former Byzantium, developed the Byzantine form of art, from a combination of Greek and Persian influences. Mosaics introduced as interior decorations and representations of divine beings, though forbidden in the religion of Semitic peoples, were here allowed. In 326 Constantine erected opposite his palace a basilica which he dedicated to wisdom and called after Santa Sophia. This was burned twice and finally rebuilt by Justinian in the sixth century, and practically as it is today, has served as a model for all Byzantine churches, of which the best known is St. Marks in Venice. Justinian seems to have been interested in gardening, for we read of his balcony garden, and that he introduced the mulberry tree from China for the sake of the silk industry.

Of all the saints, Saint Benedict was the most interesting to garden lovers for the reason that he made work in the garden one of the rules of his order.

As the son of noble parents, he was educated in Rome. At fifteen he had become disgusted with the evil he saw about him and chose to live the life of a hermit, spending three years in a cave at Mount Subiaco, a wild place in one of the loveliest mountain regions of Italy. His fame as a wonder worker drew many people about him, among them other hermits who finally begged him to become their head. He accepted reluctantly, and in a short time his followers, finding his way of life too hard, put poison in his cup of wine. St. Benedict made the sign of the cross over it and the cup fell in pieces. He then returned to his cave but crowds of hermits continued to gather round him.

Nearby, as the crow flies, is Monte Casino, where as late as the sixth century stood a temple to Apollo. St. Benedict took it upon himself to destroy it. In its place he erected two Christian chapels, and after converting the pagans to Christianity, established there the Benedictine Order.

Another rich young man who was drawn to the religious life gave his villa on the Caelian hill to the order for a monastery and hospital. He himself lived in a cell as a Benedictine monk, there spending his time in study, until in the year 590 he was called to be Pope and became known as Gregory the Great.

It was a terrible time. Totilla's reign had laid waste the cities of Italy; incessant rain had flooded the country, destroying the crops, and worst of all the plague had grievously reduced the population of many cities. Gregory then came forth from his seclusion to the rescue of his fellow citizens. He gave his inheritance of vast territories in the glorious hill country between Subiaco and Palestrina to the Benedictines, his friend Benedict was chosen Abbot of the order thus founded.

The rule of the Benedictines was severe. To the three vows of Obedience, Poverty and Chastity, St. Benedict added a fourth, that of Stability. He also instituted the rule of manual labor for seven hours a day. This meant gardening and for centuries the Christian monks were the guardians of the art of garden making in the western world.

At first the monastic life consisted of a community of contemplatives living on the property of some noble lord who protected them. Often the private temples of noble pagans were used as Christian churches and became the centers of monastic groups. We often find them in Italian monasteries forming one side of the cloister. According to the Eastern custom in building, the rooms opened from a roofless court. This was sometimes surrounded on the inside by a covered walk, to which was given the name of cloister,—an extremely advantageous form of architecture for monastic life. Here the monks would walk and meditate. The open space became the cloister garth, divided by paths crossing in the center. Here the monks tilled the soil, raising their herbs and concocting their cordials, tending their flowers and making their perfumes. In the cloister garth there was always a well, most carefully guarded for religious purposes as well as for secular uses. Sometimes the cloister garth was all green and was called Paradise.

As the monastic orders increased in wealth and importance the life changed. The hours of out-of-door labor were lessened and more time was given to the copying of manuscripts.

Into the monasteries travellers would come bringing news and tales of adventure. One would tell of the prophet, Mohammed, whose followers were carrying the new religion along both sides of the Mediterranean, building temples which they called mosques, and palaces like those of the East. Before the mosques, they said, were great courts like the cloisters of the Christians, only in place of the well there was the Pool of Purification where every Mohammedan must bathe his feet before entering the temple. Within the enclosures were high towers built of brick laid in patterned design with marvelous green and blue tiles let in; and from these the muezzin called all to prayer.

During the twelfth century the absorbing interest was the great adventure of the Crusades. Their object was to wrest the holy city of Jerusalem from the power of the Turk. The result was a great loss of life, the continued rule of the hated Turk, and the re-opening of the East to the West. The survivors brought home works of art and priceless manuscripts which were taken to the monasteries to be copied and studied. The Crusades also gave a tremendous impetus to the art of gardening. The Crusaders saw gardens of a splendor beyond their wildest dreams. The descriptions they brought home showed that the gardens in the East had changed very little since the days of Alexander.

The management of a monastery was no sinecure. The convent or body of individuals who composed the religious community, consisted of cloistered monks, professed brethren, lay and clerical, clerks, novices, artificers, and servants, all under the Abbot. The servants and artificers came from the lower ranks of society and were often villagers more pagan than Christian. The novices usually came from noble families. All the rest were of different degrees of rank and social position. The children of the poor were received into monastic schools where in addition to the ordinary education they were taught manners. According to an old rhyme minute directions for proper deportment were included in the school curriculum.*

The whole convent was under the management of the Abbot who was bound, however, to govern according to the rule of the order. He did not live in common with his monks but had a separate house of his own with a private chapel. His duty was to set an example, to preach to and confess them and see that they kept the rule. Later, houses for women were added, under an Abbess who held an exalted position equal to the Abbot's.

In addition to his religious duties the Abbot had many secular ones. There were properties of his own and of the convent far and near which required visiting, involving the Abbot in the duties of a feudal lord. Then too he had to act the part of host, and entertain all guests of noble rank, for this was in the days when the convents took the place of hotels and anyone was welcome there.

The commoners were entertained in the Guest House.

An Abbot was usually of the nobility and entertained according to his rank, although often living on very simple fare himself. Subject to him were a number of officials, the prior, the precentor, the cellerer, the sacrist, the hospitaller, and many more. Every abbey had an infirmary with its own kitchen and chapel and a garden where the monks cultivated herbs and flowers to delight the eye of the convalescent. They also had

---

*Professor Walsh gives in the appendix of "The Thirteenth, the Greatest of Centuries," a delightful poem on manners which was part of the Monastic School curriculum.

vegetable gardens and extensive orchards and vineyards; poultry houses, and houses for the gardener and poultry keeper. In fact they were great farmers. It is said that even St. Benedict lent a hand in bringing in the hay when a shower threatened. The convent lands extended over vast tracts in many parts of Europe and everywhere much attention was paid to their forests. We are told, too, that their tenantry were happy and prosperous. In times of trouble when warfare was practically incessant, the convents were sought for refuge and the doors were never closed.

At Monte Casino it was visiting day for the Abbot, day of all others that he liked best. The monks came shivering into the chapel at sunrise, and the Abbot read the inspiring service with a new ring in his voice. After his morning meal (if we can call it that) he gave his parting instructions to the prior who would take his place during his absence, which this time would be longer than usual.

A mule was brought round and the Abbot was off, down the steep path to the road that comes from Rome and goes to the sea. He looked with longing eyes to the right, toward Rome, but turned to the left, until he came to a wood road which led again to the mountains. Here it was wilder. The fields were bright with anemones, and the hillsides gold with genesta. Not a cloud was in the sky. The mule ambled on and the Abbot began to hum a Gregorian chant. At nine o'clock, or, as he would have said, Terce, he dismounted and recited the service of the day and hour. Then on again until noon, when according to the rule he should have concentrated on the painful thought of Christ being nailed to the cross. The Abbot dismounted and drew from his habit a crucifix of ivory fashioned in the Byzantine manner. Standing against the cross, the Christ was represented as a strong young man clothed in a seamless tunic, the arms stretched on the arms of the cross, his hands in the attitude of benediction, his head rising above the cross. The face was serene like a Greek statue with no sign of physical agony. The Abbot loved it. To him it suggested the good shepherd. The Abbot was troubled by the new art representing the dead Christ, nailed to the cross, an agonized, emaciated man, as the emblem of Christian faith. Steeped in Byzantine art he could not bear the modern realism. For himself he preferred the Greek monogram on the cross to this painful figure. The crucifix meant, or should mean, triumph and victory, the victory of the divine over the material.

Today he couldn't think of the agony. It was spring, all nature was alive; winter, the path to spring, had passed and spring triumphant brought light and warmth to the earth and courage to the soul. Christ told his disciples that he came to bring light to the world. He must try to keep this message alive and teach his disciples this. He wished there might be at Monte Casino one of those Byzantine mosaics where Christ triumphant dominates the church with a tremendous sense of divine power. You could not get away from it, divine power, that unseen something which helps us all to rise above the material side of life into the serenity of spiritual victory.

The mule, meanwhile, had made the most of her opportunity and found moss to roll in and grass to feed on, and seemed to sense the reality that their journey is almost ended. The path led a little higher up to an anchorite's cell, where a former student of Monte Casino was then leading the life of a hermit. He and the Abbot were great friends and had not been together for a long time. They talked late into the night. The younger one told his superior that he could not make up his mind to enter the monastic order. Nor was he sure that he wanted to become a priest. Study appealed to him, or at least to one side of him, but the other side loved freedom, and freedom involved war which he hated. He wanted peace and wanted to be of use in the world.

He told of an experience he had had when he was a little child in a church, a dark little church, when a heavy shower came up and you could scarcely see the altar. Friar Giocchino, an old, old monk was preaching when suddenly the clouds broke away and the sun shone, flooding the doorway with light. The friar stopped his preaching and intoned the Veni Creatore, and then led his congregation out in the open to gaze upon the glory of the heavens. He would like to be such a man.

The Abbot told him that Father Giocchino was a Benedictine monk who, through his whole life, had been subjected to the strictest rule. Before entering the order he had lived in solitude for forty days in a cave on Mount Tabor. Later he founded the little Abbey of dei Fiori in the Calabrian mountains. Receiving apocalyptic visions, he travelled through Italy proclaiming three revelations: the first, covering the years from Adam to Christ, had been the way of the flesh; the second, from Christ to St. Benedict, was divided between the flesh and the spirit; the third would be proclaimed by the monks, of whom St. Benedict would be the first and chief. To him the three ages were as starlight, dawn, and the full sunlight of God: as the winter, the spring, and the glorious summer: or as three plants, one bearing nettles, the second roses, the third lilies. The first age is that of the Father, creator of everything in Heaven and Earth; the second of the Son, who veiled himself within our flesh; the third, that of the spirit of God, which offers us liberty because it is love. A marvelous man, Fra Giocchino, (now known as Abbot Joachim), a wonderful personality. The anchorite sighed and said he feared he had aimed too high. The Abbot then spoke seriously of the protection of an order in these troublous times, and the inspiration of community association; but he thought of his own rebellion to monastic life.

The young brother then asked if the Abbot remembered the rich young Francis of Assisi who once stopped for a few days at the convent on his way to Rome. Had he heard that he had given up his gay life and become religious, espousing Lady Poverty? Yes, the Abbot had heard of this change of life and had been to see him in Assisi where he found him feeding his birds and tending his flowers, preaching and living by word and deed the gospel of love. He had tremendous power of imagination and drew all the shy little animals of the forest to him. Like the Good Shepherd he carried the lambs in his arms. The birds sang to him as to no one else. The flowers seemed to spring up out of the ground as he walked through the meadows. Already he had many followers. While he did not belong to the Benedictine order he followed the rule of Poverty, Obedience and Chastity. The Abbot thought he would surely be a leader, but probably would never be a cloistered monk or student. The anchorite said he would like to join him but was not sure he had the vocation. Like Francis he loved the birds, the beasts, and the flowers, and every thing that God had made. Was it necessary to belong to an order to follow Christ? Christ himself belonged to no order, why should his disciple? He was hoping and praying for a vision or message from the Lord to help him decide on his next step. The Abbot assured him that the light would come, and he hoped that he would be led to enter the Benedictine order. He reminded him that he belonged to a family of able craftsmen. Why not come back to Monte Casino and help in these arts. Calls were coming from churches all over the world for copies of the Sacred Scripture. He must surely remember the copy of the Lindesfarne Gospels that Pope Innocent had loaned to the Abbey, and no one was better qualified to copy the illuminations in that rare book than he. Then, too, artisans must be trained to paint the story of the life of Jesus Christ on the walls of the churches the Holy Father was doing his utmost to rebuild and restore. Perhaps he might be sent to Rome to work there. There was much work to be done, and he must remember that Solitude and Contemplation should lead to service. Taking the young hermit by the hand, he led him out into the starlight where "the heavens declare the glory of God." Together they prayed for light.

The next day after Lauds he again mounted the faithful mule and set out over the hills to the little village of Sermonetta where his brother was in charge of an estate of the Caetani. He arrived in time for lunch, a simple meal which they ate on the terrace, overlooking the Pontine Marshes with the picturesque Abbey church of Ninfa just below them. The brother and his family were very dear to the Abbot. He and his brother talked agriculture; the latest improvements in fertilizers; the trimming of the vines; intensive farming. For all of these the Benedictines were famous, the great properties in Subiaco and Monte Casino giving opportunity for experimental work. The farmer brother said he had bought a fine pair of white oxen and a new cart, and now could send his wine to Rome.

The lady of the castle insisted that the Abbot should go with her into her little enclosed garden, her "giardino secreto," in which she worked herself. She showed how the path divided it into two equal parts; one contained her herbs and flowers to make nosegaies and garlands of, as march violets, gilleflowers, marigolds, and she calls it the 'nosegaie garden,' because her seeds came from England. The other part of the garden is filled with all other sweet smelling herbs, as southern-wood, wormwood, rosemary, camomile, ringwort, sweet balm, anis, horehound, and other 'such like,' which she calls her garden for 'herbs of good smell.' She used rosemary for her garden borders, being near enough to the sea for it to thrive, though too near for box borders. She also used her herbs for a family medicine closet and gave a recipe or two to her brother-in-law to take back to the monks in his monastery. She told him that for gout he must make a liniment of rosemary, and for bronchial troubles there was nothing like it mixed with honey. She took a natural pride in her rose arbors; and in her vineyards that from over the wall sent forth their tender shoots of green. The cherries and plums were then in flower. They returned to the house where she gave him a stole made with her own hands; she having been taught the art by a nun in the French monastery at Poitiers. The design was taken from the famous cope of Ascoli, and consisted in heraldic figures enclosed in circles of conventional flowers and birds. It was laid out in a series of interlacing squares containing a heraldic design of some scriptural meaning. The embroidery was executed on a flat surface and then bossed up to look like bas-relief, the embossing done by pressing a heated metal knob into the work at such points as needed to be emphasized. The stitches ran in zigzag and all slanted from the center outward. The wheeled cherubim were marvelous! The Abbot was overcome by delight with the gift and assured her it would be much appreciated at Monte Casino, and he would wear it on festival days.

The countess spoke of the need of the cloistered life for the women of Italy. She told of the delightful atmosphere in the French Abbey of Poitiers where she had been educated. She told how it had been established in the time of St. Benedict by a royal lady, St. Radegund, who had retreated from the world. There she cultivated her garden in peace and grew flowers for the service of God. The poet Fortunatus was a great friend of hers and she used to send him presents of food always accompanied by flowers. Once he dined with her and she had the dishes wreathed with flowers and roses lying on the table cloth, while garlands hung on the refectory walls in the fashion of the ancients. Such a profusion of flowers meant a large garden and skillful culture.

The Abbot was much taken with the story and told his sister that very recently Brother Francis of Assisi had established a nunnery for the order of Sister Clare and had given them the little church and monastic buildings of St. Damien. He advised her to go there and see it very soon. Sister Clare had a dear little garden full of sweet smelling herbs, lilies and roses. One could look down on it from a charming loggia in the convent and see way beyond it to the Umbrian plain. The convent itself was charmingly situated on a hillside in the midst of an olive orchard through which wound a path uphill to Assisi, a most interesting place. Really she must go there.

The next day the Abbot went to the little Abbey Church of Ninfa, already falling into decay on account of the malaria then ravaging the Pontine Marshes which in the old Roman days had been such splendid grain fields. He told the prior of Ninfa that he was soon going to Rome to visit the new hospital of the Holy Spirit and see if he could not get a man learned in the modern ways of curative medicine to come down to this stricken country and make the people well.

He went on to the Abbey of Fossanova. One of his students with a number of followers had left the order of Benedictines and joined the reformed order of Cistercians, and was now head of this beautiful abbey. The church was a fine example of the new style of architecture called Gothic. The refectory was also Gothic in design but the gem of the place was the cloister with its twisted columns of Cosmati inlays, enclosing a garden full of roses and lilies the joy and pride of monks. The Abbot reaching Fossanova just as the monthly Fair was breaking up was welcomed by the crowd waving the branches of almond blossoms which had decorated their booths built around the square in front of the new church. The men were collecting the cattle and goats frightened by the change of masters which were consequently bellowing and bucking; chickens tied by their legs were flapping their wings in protest; and children, tired to death, clung to their mothers' petticoats. The young girls wore new copertas, gay with floral designs, bought from pedlars just home from the East. A group of musicians, a harpist, a flutist and a player on the lyre started the young people singing and dancing in a place cleared for them in the square.

The hour of Vespers came and into the church the tired people flocked. From the chancel the Abbot looked down on a motley crowd. The setting sun streaming in through the rose window shed its light on the little babies asleep in their mothers' arms. The gay copertas made bright spots in the sombre church.

The Abbot led the choir in the chanting of the hymns and the words and music brought peace and comfort to the tired congregation. Collecting their burdens the crowd started on its homeward way.

Across a garden of orange and lemon trees the Abbot took his way to the monastic buildings where the monks had their cells.

After Terce, the following morning, the monks and friars marched to the chapter house where the Abbot spoke to them telling the story of the making of the Ark according to the directions of Jehovah given to Moses. Every minute detail was planned for even to the cups for the six-branched candlestick which was to stand on the table before the Ark; the cups were to be made like the almond blossoms, and the whole candlestick to be made of one piece of gold beaten into shape—and now on the altar of their own church the furnishings were symbolic of this ancient Ark made for the guarding of the Holy Law. He told how the curtains were to be woven of fine linen with winged cherubim worked in by skillful workmen. He then went on to tell, in contrast to all this splendour, of the new brotherhood of Mendicant Friars, who were working to establish the Kingdom of Heaven here among men, saluting each other when they met with a holy kiss and the words, "Pax et Bonum." Here in this quiet place the monks could join in this work with their prayers and holy living in their cloistered life away from the tumult of the world. A beautiful cloister filled with flowers did not shut out the pulse or breath of life. It achieved its joy by inclusion, not by exclusion. It offers its loveliness to every eye, and its peace to every soul.

The rest of the morning was filled with business relative to the farm as well as to the spiritual life of the

Abbey. Several of the monks had to be reprimanded for inattention to the rule. In the afternoon after Primes the Abbot joined the monks in the cloister where special dispensation was given to them allowing them to talk with the Abbot. They were busy making their cordials and perfumes, and glad enough to talk while they worked.

One told of a brother who was suffering from palsy and he did wish he had some of those aspen leaves which when they were shaking would cure him. Another had nettle rash and was making nettle tea to cure that. Several were concocting a heart restorative with the heart-shaped leaves of the wood sorrel. Like the Greeks and the Romans they spoke of the lily as the symbol of purity and the oak as the symbol of strength.

They told the Abbot how the farmers calculated their harvests in advance by the size of the arum lily stem when it appeared in the spring. The arum lily, they said, came from the rod brought back to Moses from the land of milk and honey; when he stuck it in the ground it came up as a lily. The Abbot told them that it was now associated with the Lord's crucifixion. The purple spots on the leaves came from drops of blood which had fallen from the wounds of Christ and covered the breast of a bird trying to remove the nails from His hands and feet. Later it had alighted on the leaves of the lily, staining them with crimson. These Cistercian monks loved their garden just as much as the Benedictines did, and the prior related a legend of one brother who had climbed to the very top rung of the ladder of virtue, but then looked behind him, and beheld his flowery garden and plunged headlong into his rose bed, because he could not bear to leave it even for a heavenly paradise.

The monks were much interested in the meaning of flowers. Roses and lilies they especially loved, for they were symbols of Mary, and were worn as the crown of martyrdom. A guest who was present spoke of the many legends of the rosemary: how the Greeks and Romans had made garlands of it to crown the guest of honor at their feasts, and had burned it as incense at many of their religious ceremonies. During the Shepherds' Festival held in April to celebrate the founding of Rome by shepherds and husbandmen, rosemary and laurel were burned in large quantities that the smoke might purify the sacred groves and fountains from the pollution of flocks and herds. Another guest, who had come from Britain, said that it was customary in the early days in England for a bride to wear sprays of rosemary wound in her bridal wreath by some member of her family to remind her that she should take to her new home memories of the one she was leaving. Rosemary was also used by the Britons in the observance of Christmas, for the wassail bowl was wreathed with rosemary and the boar's head was trimmed with it. Another guest remarked that its association with Christmas might be explained by an old Spanish tradition, that when Mary was fleeing with her child from Herod's soldiers, some plants rustled, betraying the travelers; but a tall rosemary bush stretched out its arms and they found refuge in its thick foliage. There was also a legend that the linen and little frocks of Jesus were spread upon a rosemary bush to dry, and when Mary came to get them she found them hanging on a sunbeam. Thus it became Mary's rose and was thought to bring peace and goodwill to every family who numbered it among their Christmas adornments.*

---

*On Ascension Day it is still used with the genesta and lily in the wreaths that adorn the wayside shrines or in garlands that decorate the houses in the little villages of rural districts, a custom very like the old pagan festival of Persephone bringing back the flowers of Spring.

Reluctantly the Abbot left this charming abbey, surrounded by its protecting mountains. How gloriously the spring was coming to the earth. He wanted to go to Rome to see the new hospital there, but no, it was time to plant the corn, and almost time for the little chicks to hatch and he was not sure of his new poultry man. No, he could not go to Rome this time. He took his way back by the highway. He had had his mountain holiday.

The Abbot returned to his duties at Monte Casino and the days and years passed by in the old routine. Gradually the manual labor in the fields was relegated to lay brethren. The monks devoted their time to copying manuscripts, illustrating them with miniature pictures of their daily lives.

Changes came. The kindly Abbot, the saintly Francis, Pope Innocent III. have gone to the world of their dreams and aspirations. Of the trio, St. Francis lives in unfading memory as prophet of a new age. The teaching of his life is summed up in the little flowers which bloom perpetually in the hearts of his followers.

On the Umbrian Hills above Assisi, a country boy watched his father's sheep. To pass the time he scratched pictures on the stones. The great Cimabue found him and taught him the rudiments of drawing and painting, and the boy became the painter, Giotto. On the walls of the new church over the tomb of St. Francis he painted the life of the saint. They tell the story well and show Giotto to have broken through the Byzantine tradition. The picture of St. Francis standing in his garden feeding the birds is one of the earliest examples of a landscape background. He paints the Virgin riding on a mule holding in her arms the little child Jesus while Joseph walks behind them. They are fleeing to Egypt, and the surrounding scene is charmingly real. For the frescoes of the Lower Church Giotto drew upon Dante for the great and mysterious symbolism of the Divine Comedy. Giotto traced in the picture of Chastity the austere figure of Dante and there is the singer of the Inferno kneeling at the feet of St. Francis, covered with his great cloak whose pointed hood hangs down almost to his feet.

The Benedictine monasteries soon ceased to be the communities of self-denying ascetics which originally they had been. Their general character became that of wealthy and learned bodies influential because of possessions and still more because they were guardians of nearly all the literature, art, and science of the period. The library at Monte Casino increased rapidly. The reputation of the monks as good craftsmen brought many manuscripts to their door.

One visitor came from Persia with a book. He told the Abbot it was written in a little garden which opened out of a court in which was the shrine of a saint. There the great poet Omar Khayyam passed many happy days with his beloved Saki. There he gathered about him poets, philosophers, and statesmen who sought his wisdom. There he wrote and read his Rubaiyat in the midst of roses, their petals falling on the grave of his beloved Saki by whose side he too was soon laid away.

Manuscripts of all kinds were copied in the monasteries. The French tale of Aucassin and Nicolette was in great demand. One imagines that possibly the monks, especially the novices, found it very diverting, more so than the scientific works of Albertus Magnus and his pupil Roger Bacon. The three books most read in the thirteenth century, apart from the Bible were Reynard the Fox, the Golden Legend, and The Romaunt of the

Rose. This latter was beautifully illustrated with pictures of quaint little enclosed gardens.

At the close of the century our path through cloistered gardens brings us to Dante, the divine poet of all ages. Steeped in the pagan myths, as well as in mediaeval mysticism, he carries one through the Inferno, where light shineth not, into the Purgatorio where one's face is toward the light. He leads on through the visions of Ezekiel and St. John to the Earthly Paradise, full of a diversity of tender blossoms, where he meets Matilda, "a lady solitary, who went along singing and culling flower after flower, wherewith all her path was painted .... She smiled from the right bank opposite, gathering more flowers with her hands, which the high land bears without seed... And Lo, a sudden brightness flooded on all sides the great forest, such that it set me in doubt if 'twere lightning. But since lightning ceases even as it cometh, and that enduring, brighter and brighter shone, in my mind I said, 'What is this?' "
... Some of us, like Virgil, must leave him in the terrestrial Paradise. Our imagination cannot follow him into the radiance of the Paradiso.

Could there be any greater contrast than the beginning and end of the thirteenth century? St. Francis at the beginning, feeding his birds and tending his flowers, doing the little nameless things of life that tell of the love of God and love to man. Pax et Bonum his motto, the Canticle to the Sun his creed; and Dante's Apotheosis of Mediaeval Theology and Mysticism at the end!

In looking back over the thirteenth century it stands out in my mind as the Portico to the Renaissance. In place of the six columns of the Greek temple stand six great personalities of modern thought: St. Francis and

Giotto, the realists; Albertus Magnus, the scientist; Marco Polo, the adventurer; St. Thomas Aquinas, the great intellectual, who summed up for all time the teaching of mediaeval mysticism; and Dante, the great poet who brought its thought to the people.

"One universal, animating soul quickens, unites, and mingles with the whole."

CHAPTER V

A PATH OF ROMANCE AND POETRY

On the front page of an old book about gardens the designers wrote as a heraldic legend above three small symbolical flower beds,

"For Health, For Goodness, For Beauty."

CHAPTER V

WHILE the monks were living their secluded lives in flowery cloisters, copying immortal literature, adventurous spirits were taking advantage of the Crusades to tread unknown or at least forgotten paths leading back to the East. From there had come, at the close of the twelfth century, a letter to the crowned heads of Europe —a most extraordinary letter from a most extraordinary man, Prester John, who claimed to be a powerful Christian Emperor in Abyssinia, and has since been thought to belong to that branch of the Christian Church founded by Nestorius, a priest of Antioch, in the fifth century.

In the letter he claimed to be a priest "by the almighty power of God and the might of our Lord Jesus Christ." Apparently the letter was to acknowledge presents and to accompany gifts from his kingdom, which he then goes on to describe. "In the Indies our magnificence rules and our land extends beyond India toward Babylon near the Tower of Babel. The land is the home of every known animal, it streams with honey and overflows with milk. In one region grows no poisonous herb, nor does a querulous frog ever quack in it, no scorpion exists, nor does the serpent glide amongst the grass, nor can any poisonous animals exist in it. Among the heathen, flows through a certain province the river Indus; encircling Paradise, it spreads its arms in manifold windings through the entire province. Here are found all the precious stones—and the plant Assidos which, when worn by anyone, protects him from the evil spirit." In another province every kind of pepper is gathered, which is exchanged for corn and bread, leather and cloth. "At the foot of Mount Olympus bubbles up a spring which changes its flavour hour by hour, night and day, and the spring is scarce three days journey from Paradise. If anyone taste thrice of the fountain, from that day he will feel no fatigue, but will as long as he lives be as a man of thirty years."—And the letter goes on describing many more marvels, among them another fountain "of singular virtue which purges Christians and would-be Christians from all transgressions. The water stands four inches high in a hollow stone shaped like a mussel shell. Two saintly old men watch by it and ask the comers whether they are Christians or about to become Christians; then whether they desire healing with all their hearts. If they have answered well they are bidden to lay aside their garments and step into the mussel. If what they said be true, then the water begins to rise and gush over their heads; thrice does the water thus lift itself, and everyone who has entered the mussel, leaves it cured of every complaint."*

Prester John was killed by Genghis Khan who during the twelfth century had led his conquering hordes of Tartars across Asia, from the walls of China to the gates of Russia, building as he went, across the desert, palaces at intervals for the accommodation of his army. By the thirteenth century his existence was doubted by many, but Marco Polo believed in him. His desire to find the fabulous kingdom was a strong reason for joining his uncle and father on their second expedition to the East. He never did find it, though he believed he had identified Prester John with Unk Khan, a famous shepherd. He did, however, acquire an inside knowledge of China, where for a number of years he was the hon-

---

*Curious Myths of the Middle Ages.   S. Baring Gould.   Courtesy of Longmans, Green & Co.

ored guest of Kublai Khan, grandson of Genghis Khan, to whom he is supposed to have given valuable suggestions for governing and by whom he was made ruler of a Chinese province. To Marco Polo, the new capital of Kublai Khan seemed the most beautiful place in the world. It was bounded on one side by the river Hsi-hu or Western Lake, which has always been considered by the Chinese as the loveliest landscape in the kingdom. The lake which stretched the length of the city was dotted with pleasure boats from which one had a magnificent view of palaces, temples and gardens filled with fine old trees.

Even in Marco Polo's time many of these places had begun to run down owing to the curious etiquette of Chinese emperors and prominent citizens which forbids them to live in the house of an ancestor. Each new dynasty was obliged to make a new capital which became thereby the center of art and culture. Although the old palaces were supposed to be kept up as occasional residences for the traveling emperor, they soon fell into disrepair.

In Marco Polo's description of the palace of Kublai Khan, he says that the footpaths were raised and paved so that the water would run off and they would never be dirty. In the garden there was an artificial mound made of the earth dug out to create a lake. The mound was a mile square at its base and rose a hundred feet. On it were planted trees which the Emperor had collected from all parts of his kingdom and which had been brought there by elephants. It was covered with green earth and called the Green Hill. On the top there was a palace, green inside and out. Between the mound and a palace built for his son, lay a lake over which a bridge passed connecting the two palaces.

The Chinese gardens are laid out according to rule, to propitiate the "kindly deities" and keep away the evil spirits; for this reason the roofs of the pagodas have an upward curve in order that the spirits may not descend to the ground. A peculiar reverence is shown for stones and mountains and flowing water is symbolized by the dragon, the bringer of good fortune. The law of contrasts is observed with marked success. In the scenery of a garden the smiling landscape needs for contrast some dark note, like an overhanging rock, a deformed tree, broken by the storm, dark hollows or foaming water falls. From ancient Chinese poetry we have word pictures of gardens, real or imaginary. From the pen of the great poet, Li-Tai-po in the eighth century we have several descriptions of gardens. The following suggests the garden of Kublai Khan who lived three or four centuries later and for which the poem may have served as a model.

> "In the middle of the lake we made
> Is a porcelain house all green and white.
> Thither we walk on a bridge of jade
>
> "Arched like the back of a tiger.
> In this pavilion sit our friends,
> In garments light, and drink their wine,
> With merry talk, or writing verse,
> Their heavy headgear they discard,
> And turn their sleeves a little up.
>
> "And in the lake a little bridge appears,
> A crescent moon of jade, turned upside down
> So standing on their heads, our friends are seen
> In lightest garments clad, and drink their wine
> In a porcelain house—"*

---

*Marie Luise Gothein. History of Garden Art. Courtesy of E. P. Dutton & Co.

The great statesman, Hsi-Ma-Kuang, belongs to this century. He was a man of learning, and from his pen we have a description of his country home.

"Other palaces may be built, wherein to escape from grief or to subdue the vanities of life, but I have built a hermitage, where at my leisure I may find repose and hold converse with my friends. Twenty acres are all the space I need. In the middle is a large summer house where I have brought together my five thousand books, so as to consult the wisdom therein, and to hold converse with antiquity. On the south side there is a pavilion in the middle of the water, by whose sides runs a stream that flows down the hill on the east. The waters make a deep pond, whence they part in five branches like a leopard's claws; numbers of swans swim there and are always playing about. At the border of the first stream, which falls in cascades, there stands a steep rock with overhanging top like an elephant's trunk, at the summit stands a pleasant open pavilion where people can rest, and wherein they can enjoy any morning the red sunrise. The second arm is divided after a few feet into two canals, which twist and turn about the gallery, bordered by a double terrace. The Eastern arm turns backward toward the north, beside the arch of a pillared hall, which stands in an isolated position, and is thus made into an island. The shores of this island are covered with sand, shells, and pebbles of different colors, one part of it is planted with evergreen trees. There is also a hut made of straw and rush, just like a fisherman's hut. The two other arms seem alternately fleeing and pursuing, for they follow the turns of a flowery meadow, and keep it fresh. They often overflow their bed, and make little pools, which are edged with soft grass; then they escape into the meadow, and flow on in narrow canals which disperse in a labyrinth of rocks that hinder their course, confine them, and break them. Hence they burst forth in foaming silver waves, and so pursue their proper course. There are several pavilions on the north of a large summer house, scattered about here and there; some of them are on hills, one above the other, standing like a mother among her children, while others are built on the slopes; several of them are in little gaps made by the hills, and only half of them can be seen, the whole region is overshadowed by a forest of bamboos, intersected by sandy foot paths, where the sun may never penetrate. Towards the east there is a little level of irregular shapes, protected from the cold north winds by a cedar wood. All the valleys are full of sweet smelling plants, medicinal herbs, bushes and flowers. In this lovely place there is always spring, at the edge of the horizon there is a copse of pomegranates, citrons, and oranges, always in flower and in fruit. In the middle there is a green pavilion to which one mounts by an imperceptible slope along several spiral paths, which become narrower as they get near the top. The paths on this hill are bordered by grass, and tempt one to sit down from time to time, so as to enjoy the view from every side. On the west, one walk of weeping willows leads to the bank of the river, which comes down from the top of a rock covered with ivy and wild flowers of all kinds and colors. All round there are rocks piled anyhow, with an odd effect rather like that of an amphitheatre! Right on the ground there is a deep grotto, which gets wider the farther one goes, and makes a kind of irregular room with an arched ceiling. The light comes in through a somewhat larger opening hung around with wild vines and honeysuckles. Rocks serve as seats, and one gets protection in the blazing dog days by going into the alcoves and sitting there. A small stream comes out on one side and fills the hollow of a great stone, and then it drops out in little trickles to the floor, winding about in the cracks and fissures till it falls into a reservoir bath. This basin has more depth when it reaches an arch, where it makes a little turn and flows into a pond, which is down at the bottom of the grotto. This pond leaves only a little foot path between the shapeless rocks, which are oddly heaped together in piles all around. A whole family of rabbits is established among them, terrifying the fishes in the lake and in turn terrified by them. What an enchanting spot this hermitage is! The second pond has little sedgy islands on it, the larger ones full of birds of every kind and bird houses. The way to get from one to the other is by the big stones that stick out of the water or by the small wooden bridges that are scattered about, some of them are arched, some in straight lines or zigzags, according to the space that has to be filled up. When the water lilies near the bank are in full bloom, the pond seems to be wreathed in purple or scarlet, like the edge of the southern sea when the sun rises. Pedestrians must make up their minds whether to go back the same way they came, or to climb up the rocks that close in the place on every side. Nature intended that these rocks should be approachable from one end only of the pond. They seem to be fastened together where the waters have opened up a thoroughfare among the willows that stand between them, breaking through on the other side, and forcing their way with a roar. Old fir trees conceal the dip, and nothing can be seen among their top branches but the stones that have become imbedded in a groove or in some broken tree trunks. Leading up the summit of this rocky wall, there is a steep narrow stairway; and this has been chipped out with a hatchet; the mark of the blows is still visible. The pavilion which is set up here as a resting place is quite simple, but it is remarkable for its view of a wide plain, where the river Kiang follows a serpentine course in the rice fields."*

In the latter years of the Sung Dynasty, blue and white china with the familiar design of the willow and bridge made its appearance. The frequent use of floral designs and pictures of Chinese grandees in their gardens show the love the Chinese people had for growing things. In 1280 Kublai Khan was proclaimed emperor of all China. Under him the doors of China were opened to foreigners, who flocked there over the trade routes made safe by his predecessors. The Mongolian Empire lasted only a hundred years; then the Ming dynasty came back in great power.

In China, culture and technique went hand in hand. From childhood the Chinese were trained in the use of the brush and taught the laws of perspective. There are a few ancient paintings in existence which impress one by the balance of their composition and their exquisite sense of perspective. There is in them a mysterious feeling of mistiness, a softness of color that cannot be described. They show the extensive use of water in the garden, islands topped with pagodas, and connected by bridges, of various shapes, and all painted with delicious soft color. The pagoda roofs of the royal palaces are of golden tiles which with the red walls, softened by time to a beautiful rose, give a purple color to the city when seen from a distance.

The Imperial Palaces, compared to European palaces are small, and consist of numerous pavilions connected by open galleries that wind or zig-zag up and down hills, over meadows, around lakes (one at least thirty miles around), and over streams. Each pavilion

---

*Marie Luise Gothein, Vol. II. Courtesy of E. P. Dutton & Co.

has its own gardens laid out with special reference to the season of the year in which it may be occupied. A winter pavilion is protected from the north wind by a cedar grove and other evergreens and has a sunny exposure. Every variety of evergreen tree or shrub is planted for protection. The red walls give color and form a charming background to the winter foliage.

Each pavilion has several pagodas placed to command a view to be enjoyed at stated times of the day. Each garden is enclosed by its stucco wall, usually red, with green and gold mouldings. Round doors and odd shaped windows, carved like a picture frame, open to the distant view, and are so made that one can see nothing at all until the full perfection of that particular view bursts upon one.

Another unique feature is the moon gate leading from one garden enclosure to another. Here the upper part of the gate is cut out in a circle with, in many cases, a rather elaborate painted moulding as a frame for a view.

The railings of the galleries are of a simple design with panels of red lacquer carved with conventional flowers or the imperial dragon. From them steps lead up or down to pagodas screened by skillful planting, or into little enclosed gardens. The pavilions are poetically named. One is called "The Murmuring Waters of Spring," and wistaria, acacia, lilacs, and flowering fruit trees cast their color in a lake, and the song of the birds mingles with the music of the waters. Imagine, on a hot day, a pagoda in a deep grotto, into which tumble many streams over rocks, called "The Pagoda of Diffused Coolness!"

The summer pavilions make use of the water and are usually on islands, where rocky hills are artificially made with great stones worn smooth by flowing water, and planted with scrubby pines. One of these is called "The Hall of Rippling Waves." A group of peonies may give a color spot in such a garden, though the Chinese use flowers sparingly about their houses, preferring to have the building show from the ground up and depending for color on the painted walls and roofs. The columns that support the gay roofs of the pergolas are usually of red lacquer. The roofs are gold or green, or occasionally red. In one summer pavilion of white stucco there is a carved bridge beneath which a stream glides quietly by, reflecting the white bridge, the blue sky, and a border of pink lotus with its big, blue-green leaves. This might be called the "Pagoda of Placid Leisure." An autumn pavilion suggests a pagoda high up on a hill, called "The Riding on a Rainbow." Who but a Chinese poet would ever think of such names?

Chinese houses grow according to the needs of the family. A new room may be built from the corner of the house or perhaps connected with it by a gallery, forming an angle in the garden, which is effectively filled with vines and shrubs. Plants in lovely pottery vases stand about. Balconies and bamboo lattices add decorative features in addition to their use as screens. The Chinese women live in their gardens. They rarely walk, and even the men do not walk for pleasure. They all enjoy their gardens sitting down, hence the pagodas, to which lead the winding paths laid out in colored stone or mosaic tiles. Seats, usually stones, may be enjoyed at every turn in sight of a charming view. Often a favorite view is reproduced in miniature. Dwarf tree culture was a secret art, handed down from generation to generation, and regarded by the Chinese as a means of cheerfulness, destroying ennui and evil passions.

In Chinese gardens, tree and flower, stone and stream have a religious significance, and the temple symbolizes the deification of nature. The base stands for the earth; the body, water; the spire, fire; the crown, air; and the gilded ball, ether. Chinese gardens are still unique, and the story Marco Polo dictated in his prison cell at the end of the thirteenth century must indeed have seemed a fairy tale to the monks who copied it. Later travellers, however, confirmed this first account that reached the western world of the strange and wonderful gardens of the Chinese Empire. Today there is hardly a garden in this country or Europe that is not indebted to China for the plants that add charm to it. The forsythia, the acacias, the magnolias, the peonies (the parents of our modern roses, be they hybrid, tea, rambler, or polyantha), many of the azaleas and primroses, peaches, oranges, lemons and grapefruit have come to us from China.

Beside the stories that Marco Polo brought back from China, he carried in his hands two tiny seeds that developed into mighty plants, changing the whole course of life in the western world. In one hand he held a little package of gun-powder, destined to develop into the hideous machine of modern warfare. In the other was a tiny block of wood, used by the Chinese to stamp their cloth. It took nearly two hundred years for these tiny seeds to develop. Another legacy from the thirteenth century was Roger Bacon's compass which made possible the navigation of uncharted seas.

The fourteenth century began with a Jubilee Year which seemed to mark the transition from Mediaevalism to Modernism, the merging of fairy tale into history.

In this same Jubilee year, Dante was banished from Florence. Let us imagine him climbing up the steep path that leads through the old gate of San Niccolo to San Miniato, for a farewell view of his beloved city. There at his feet meandered the Arno through a fertile valley of orchards and vineyards. Picturesque walls of brick fortified with towers enclosed the city. Over them he could see the Bargello and the Palazzo Vecchio marking the streets he knew so well, where stood his own home and that of Beatrice. From near by he had watched Giotto's Campanile rising from the ground. There lay the little old Baptistry where, only a few days before, he had seen a baby boy christened, who might grow up into an Orcagna to carry on the work of Giotto. As the sun set, he could hear the bells of San Trinita and the church of the Apostoli. Would he ever meet his friends there again? Cimabue, Martini, Nicolo Pisano, an old man now? Would Giotto come back from Rome to finish the frescoes in the Santa Croce? On the surrounding hills villas were taking the place of the old castles: his little Firenze was changing and he must leave it.

Villani, the historian of those days, writes that in this year there was scarcely a Florentine who did not have a finer house in the suburbs than in the city. The burgesses as well as the nobles built their villas and planted their gardens, first of vegetables, fruits, and vineyards, and then of herbs and flowers. In his book on husbandry are many plans for gardens similar to those of the Roman Republic. He probably had read Pliny's letters. Contemporary with Villani was Crescentius of Bologna who also wrote about horticulture, making much of the artistic arrangements of the estates of the rich. He was particularly in favor of enclosed gardens with high walls and placing the house where it would have an unobstructed view to the "thickset" at the end of the garden, where wild animals should be kept. The garden plot should have a formal plan divided by paths with shrubberies at the side where there might be tame animals and near the palace there should be a fish pond and aviaries. He recommended the use of elms and fruit trees which must be flawless and wide apart. He was also in favor of evergreens, clipped for architectural effects.*

Throughout the fourteenth century the Italian countryside blossomed with gardens. They excelled those of every other country, and Italian gardeners went everywhere.

Petrarch and Boccacio, the great Italian writers of the century loved their gardens. Petrarch, born at Arezzo while his family were exiles from Florence, was a wanderer all his life. He spent a good part of it at Avignon, where he was connected with the ecclesiastical court. Finally, tired of the turmoil of public life, he acquired the charming villa of Vaucluse. There he himself worked in the garden, which he declared was for his own pleasure and not for the benefit of his grandsons. In his early years we hear of him in Padua where his friendship with Boccacio began.

Boccacio was sent by his father on some mercantile business to Naples. He hated the business, though it gave him the entré into royal society of King Robert's court where Italian men of letters used to gather. He shared with Petrarch an enthusiasm for Cicero and haunted the scenes, near Naples, of Virgil's life and writings. According to popular story, he went to the church of San Lorenzo one Easter Sunday and there saw for the first time Marie, the natural daughter of King Robert, and fell instantly in love with her. Though already

---
*History of Garden Art. Marie Luise Gothein. Courtesy of E. P. Dutton & Co.

married, she apparently did likewise, and in the gardens of the beautiful Rufali Palace at Ravello, the romantic love affair was carried on. In his writings she is immortalized as Fiammetta, the third in the great trilogy of adored ladies of the century.

Boccacio gave up his business and devoted himself to writing and we find him, while the great plague was devastating Florence, in a garden with a party of friends, writing the stories of the Decameron, happy and untroubled by the breath of pestilence that brooded over the city at their feet.

He tells us that his garden is on the heights of Fiesole, surrounded with meadows, with a path leading up to it. The guests were received in a fine inner court with a flower covered loggia. The garden where they went afterwards was at the side and walled in. There were broad walks inside the walls and down the middle. The paths were hedged with roses and there were many arbors covered with vines. There were oranges and citrons, and gay flowers, and a white marble well, and plenty of water to water the flowers. There were also plenty of tables and chairs for people to use when tired of dancing and singing.

A century after Villani, in the early part of the fifteenth century, Leon Battista Alberti wrote a book on architecture including the art of garden making. With him dawns the renaissance in Italy.

"Alberti was the first in any field to try to connect the present with the past. With him, the villa appears in all its beauty and gaiety. He dwells at length on the necessity of harmony, proportion and regularity. By gently rising paths one is led to the house without noticing the climb. There one is to be impressed with the beautiful view but enticed to go further. The garden is very cheerful, for melancholy is to be avoided. Dark shadows must be kept in the background. Porticoes and pergolas at the sides give protection from the hot sun, as also the cool grottos made of tufa after the fashion of the ancients. He also approved of using decorative pots for flowers, writing the master's name on the beds in box, and clipping the trees into animal shapes. Bright streams of water must run through the garden and start up unexpectedly from grottos. Cypresses with climbing ivy must be in the pleasure garden, but fruit trees and even oaks must be relegated to the kitchen garden. Comic statues may be tolerated but nothing obscene is permitted. Circles and semi-circles are considered beautiful in the courts and he desires to see them in the garden as well, and these he would have made with laurel, citron and yew with interwoven branches." *

With the rise of the Medici prosperity came to Florence. Intercourse with the East made of Cosimo the Elder an ardent student and collector of Greek art, and as patron of art he included the art of garden-making. At his Villa Careggi he established a Platonic Academy where he gathered about him Greek poets and philosophers. Besides these, artists found in him a most appreciative patron. He employed many of them to decorate his palaces and also gave a garden for the sculptors to work in near the monastery of San Marco. There Donatello's famous David was created for Cosimo's city house.

Artists were at work all over the city. Ghiberti, Brunelleschi, Massaccio, and Fillippo Lippi owed much to Cosimo. Michelozzo was busy building San Marco and the Medici palace.

---
*Marie Luise Gothein, Vol. I, p. 207. History of Garden Art. Courtesy of E. P. Dutton & Co.

In the monastery of San Marco, Fra Angelico lived and worked.

All through Florence Lucca della Robbia left his masterpieces, depicting the joy of life, the innocence of childhood, the love of mother and child, as well as the grief of the Madonna in a manner which has never been surpassed.

Those were busy, happy days in Florence. Piero il Gottoso succeeded his father and continued his patronage of art. For him Gozzoli decorated the chapel in the Riccardi Palace. In the chancel he laid the scene amidst Italian garden and woodland scenery with groups of angels passing about everywhere singing their song of "Glory to God," all turning toward the picture of the nativity. The kneeling groups are gazing at the great mystery in silent awe. Behind the principal groups, angels pick roses in the garden, birds fly about, peace and happiness reign. Surely the picture is of a dream garden.*

Botticelli owed much to Piero. He was taken in to the Medici house and encouraged by both Piero and his wife, Lucrezia Tournabuoni. Like Donatello his object was to express in art some deep thought and in a single picture he would portray the entire history of an episode. For this purpose he made use of allegory, thereby showing the Greek revival of literature at this time. He used allegory to represent in a symbolic way the episodes in current history. He also illustrated in the same manner various poems of Lorenzo the Magnificent who succeeded his father and inherited the tastes of his grandfather, continuing the building of villas and the study of Greek art, and literature. He and Poliziano both wrote a

---

*The Medici. Col. Young. Courtesy of E. P. Dutton & Co.

poetical drama in which there are lines about a garden, translated by Symonds.

Poliziano writes:

> "I went a-roaming, Maidens, one bright day,
> In a fair garden in midmonth of May
> I gazed and gazed. Hard task it were to tell
> How lovely were the roses in that hour
> One was but peeping from her verdant shell,
> And some were faded, some were scarce in flower."

And Lorenzo:

> "Red and white roses bloomed upon the spray;
> One opened, leaf by leaf, to greet the morn.
> Shyly at first, then in sweet disarray;
> Another yet a youngling, newly born,
> Scarce struggled from the bud, and there were some
> Whose petals closed them from the air forlorn;
> Another fell, and showered the grass with bloom."*

At this time the countrymen with their ploughs were constantly turning up pieces of Greek and early Roman sculpture. These were secured by the Medici, who placed them in their gardens. The artists also discovered an opening in the ruins of the Golden House of Nero through which they could crawl and copy some of the famous frescoes on the walls. A little panel, in the Naples Museum, of Flora, is very suggestive of Botticelli's painting of Spring, only it is gayer and lighter and altogether more charming. In Botticelli's "Spring" he pictures Simonetta in the character of Venus, presiding over the return of spring to Tuscany. The Graces dance before her; from out of a laurel grove at her side the three spring months, March, April and May (or it may be Zephyr, Fertility, and Flora), come bringing flowers of every hue; Mercury (Giuliano) scatters the

---
*Lorenzo the Magnificent. Horsburg. Courtesy of G. P. Putnam's Sons.

clouds of winter, and the little blind god of love aims his arrows recklessly around. Soon after the tournament, Simonetta died of consumption and Giuliano was murdered in the Pazzi conspiracy.

On Lake Garda there was a villa formerly a favorite haunt of Scipio. In the days of the Renaissance it belonged to Bronzoni and was known as San Vigilio. At the entrance there was the following inscription wherewith the Master greeted his guests.

> Whoever thou art, visiting this house
> Observe these twelve rules.

1. Honour in the sanctuary the best and highest God.
2. Leave your troubles in the town.
3. All girls must be banned.
4. Keep your servants' hands off the gardens.
5. Meals must not be luxurious.
6. Drink the cup that will quench your thirst.
7. Turn your mind to joyful things.
8. Lift your heart in honest play.
9. Fill your hands with boughs, flowers, and fruits.
10. Then go back to town and duty.
11. Let not Bronzoni's invitation bring harm to your host.
12. Let the honour of the place be its noblest law.*

The zenith of the art of the Renaissance falls between the years 1494 and 1512. Almost all of the great artists included architecture and landscape gardening in their work. Many of the gardens are still in existence and can be visited today. Edith Wharton has written such a delightful book describing them, I have nothing more to say. They certainly deserve a volume to themselves. Mrs. Aubrey le Blond's admirable guide, "Old Gardens of Italy and How to Visit Them" gives much useful information.

In Italy the word Villa includes the garden as well as

---
*Marie Luise Gothein.

the buildings, and the Renaissance landscape architects combine the two most successfully. Grand gateways framed in ornamental stone work opened into formal garden courts enclosed by high walls on three sides while on the fourth side enclosure was an ornamental balustrade over which one could look to a view or down to a lower level approached by stone steps, protected by the continuance of the balustrade, into a garden of flowers or vegetables with clipped hedges carrying out the architectural design of the walls in the garden court. Avenues of clipped ilex and laurel led to the woodland beyond.

From Italy one naturally follows the gardens into France and England, but our path leads us to the West. We go back to the Imperial Highway of the Mediterranean and follow the Moor into Spain.

CHAPTER VI

WITH THE MOORS IN SPAIN

"Roses for perfume,
 Bulbus for song,
 And the sight and sound of running water."
OLD TURKISH GARDEN MOTTO

CHAPTER VI

Leaving the Medici and their artists busily at work in Florence, we step again on the magic carpet and let it take us back over the century we have been passing in Italy. We could have spent centuries more visiting gardens there; or followed the garden way to the North with the landscape gardeners who carried Italian ideas into France. From there we could have gone on to England, and over the seas to America. Instead we take the path to the west and arrive in Spain. Ray de Gonzales de Clavijo has just returned from the East, where he represented his king at Tamerlane's celebration of his astonishing victory over the Turk. That a Tartar prince could accomplish what Christian princes for centuries had attempted and failed to do, was bewildering to the Western world.

Tamerlane's kingdom extended from the walls of China to Moscow, from the Tigris to the Adriatic. Ambassadors from twenty kingdoms had assembled to honor him. Henry IV. of England sent congratulations and Charles VI. of France sent gifts; Henry of Castile sent Ray de Gonzales who brought back a vivid description of Samarkand and its festival. He tells us the city walls were five miles in circumference and that within them the city rose on terraces. "Through a turquoise gate the visitors entered the Armenian quarter. They found themselves on the street of the saddle-makers, which was crowded with litters carrying singing girls escorted by little players and by tigers and goats with golden horns. These latter were not beasts at all but girls dressed up by skinners of the city. Elephants fought each other in the midst of Tartar princes arriving from

India, and Gobis loaded with gifts for Tamerlane. Above on the terraces rose the palaces and gardens of the Secretaries, and higher still the citadel quarter, where lived the officers of the staff. On the edge of the cliff stood the castle of the treasury, into which no visitor could enter. Near it were the Hermitage and Animal Park. In the courtyard, Gonzales was told, stood a tree with golden branches and leaves of silver. Hanging from its boughs were lustrous pearls and precious stones of every color shaped like cherries and plums. Red and green enamel birds with silver wings were hovering about as though pecking at the fruit. Under the citadel lay a public square, a rendez-vous for the great lords, a place of exchange for the merchants and one of prayer, storytelling or trading among the humble. It was always gay with streamers flying and fountains dripping."

Temples and academies, created by Tamerlane, surrounded the square and beyond there was another square for plays and festivals. On the citadel hill stood Tamerlane's palace in a walled garden. The entrance was through a high gate decorated with blue and gold glazed tiles. Here the ambassadors were met by porters, carrying imposing maces, to whom they gave their presents. Near by were six elephants with wooden castles on their backs, filled with men. The next step brought the visitors to an ante-room where Tamerlane's grandchildren in charge of an aged knight took their letters from the Ambassadors and carried them to Tamerlane. The Emperor then permitted them to enter the garden of "Heart's Delight." There at the entrance of the palace he received them, sitting crosslegged on an embroidered carpet.

The garden was square, enclosed by walls pierced on each side by a gate supported by rearing stone lions. Before Lord Tamerlane played a fountain in which red apples floated while the water was thrown high in the air. Sycamore and fruit trees were in bloom and the court was filled with both flowers and ripe fruit.

Within the courtyard gardeners from Persia were at work. Beyond a marble colonnade rose the walls of the central palace not yet finished. Skilled artists from China and Persia were working on different sections of the entrance hall, and a Hindoo was laying gilt and silver tissue on cement. The ceiling was a mass of flowers and mosaic.

On the Citadel Hill, the women of the court also had a palace in a court used for festivals. It was a wilderness of roses and tulips, with blue cornflowers in the grass. The acacia trees were in bloom and lighted with yellow lanterns, and the air was laden with the smoke of sandalwood and ambergris.*

Such is the story that Clavijo took back to Spain of the dream-city of Samarkand, built according to Tamerlane's fancy from his memory of Persian art. Though executed by artisans brought back by him from Persia, the result was Tartar, not Persian.

A visit to Spain today is bewildering and was probably just as much so in the fifteenth century. In either case we need the Magic Carpet to take us back in time, from place to place, without any hurry. We should take time to read Don Quixote and Washington Irving. Rose Standish Nichols too is a delightful companion, but her book is too heavy to carry comfortably, and should be read at home before and after the trip. She emphasizes the need of some knowledge of Persian work, for the Persians exerted an immense influence on the architecture and garden art of the world.

When the Moors first came to Spain in the eighth

---
*Tamerlane. Harold Lamb. Courtesy of Robert M. McBride & Company.

century they found Romanesque Christian Churches and castles, old Roman bridges and aqueducts, massive engineering work which we can still see in Segovia and Avila. They brought with them a new scale of color, green, red, orange, and turquoise blue. They worked with small materials like brick and tile, using them decoratively as in weaving, an art in which they excelled. They were always apt in picking up new ideas as they showed in Damascus, where they learned Byzantine art, and in Bagdad, where they learned Persian. Wherever they were pupils, they became masters.

They brought their color and their domes to Spain from Persia. Finding the round arch used everywhere, they adopted it, adding the horseshoe arch, which they had seen in Palestine and Egypt. Probably they brought it to Sicily as they did to Spain. It was in the old mosque of Damascus, and in El Aksa in Jerusalem, and in Tulun in Cairo. During the same time, the eighth and ninth centuries, the horseshoe arches were also used in the heart of Chinese Turkestan.

The Moors soon acquired most of the peninsula, which they ruled for eight centuries with great tolerance toward both Jews and Christians.

Their oldest city in Spain was Cordova, which they made their western capital, Bagdad being their capital in the East. Here the Moslem and Persian architects built or rebuilt Roman palaces on terraces above the river, laying out beautiful gardens with a marvellous system of irrigations. Mosques, baths and palaces sprang up almost over night during the reign of Abd-er-Rahman I. in the eighth century. He imported palm trees and plants, encouraging horticulture as well as agriculture. His "Court of Oranges" was the oldest enclosed garden in Spain.

Mrs. Gasquoine Hartley writes of Cordova delightfully in a little book, probably now out of print, from which I quote: She speaks of the color of the city as "A delicious play of pure color, pure sapphire sky, whitewashed walls, dazzling heat," (Alas, I saw it on a cold March day and it was all one color!) "A great dream city spread between the Sierra mountains and the river, with the whisper of water on one side and the stillness of the mountains on the other, a city of wealth," (in the tenth century) "of beauty and of glory, of learning, sending the influence of its culture like rain upon the earth. You catch the gleam of 50,000 palaces built of marble and of jasper; you note the flash of fountains of quicksilver, and hear the tinkle of water; you see the great library of Al Hakim, the wonder of the world, and the nine hundred public baths which beautified the city. Then you look into the enchanted gardens whose names speak of the sense of joy. 'The Meadow of Murmuring Waters,' 'The Garden of the Waterwheel,' what magic lingers in the suggestion of the words.

"The minarets of seven hundred mosques seem to tower proudly up, interlacing the sky, and in the distance the sunlight seems to rest and flash in gladness upon the suburb of Az-Zahra."

I am sure Mrs. Hartley must have walked on the magic carpet in Cordova. All those splendors, except the mosque and its court, the river and the mountains, have vanished. The court is still there with its oranges and lemons. Through the Puerta del Pardon still enter the women; one by one or in groups they go to the fountain, put down their copper pitchers, and cross the court to the mosque. In old times they could walk directly into the forest of columns, now there is a partition wall, and you enter through a curtain. In the court children are playing and beggars ply their trade. Mrs. Hartley sees a "band of Acolytes in scarlet cassocks come from the chancery towards the mosque making a line of flame. A sound of music comes from within. There is a church service in the mosque. Nowhere else in Cordova do the past and present seem so interfused as in this court. All the genius of the Moorish work, with its splendor of color is here. Lulled by its warmth one pauses to recall the drama of its history before entering the Mosque. There in the corner of the court stand columns of stone from the early temple of Janus, ... memory of Pagan Rome .... In the eighth century the Christian church of St. Vincent stood where now rises the mosque, —a monument of religious tolerance, one half the building consecrated to Allah, the other to the Christian God. For a number of years they were worshipped side by side, a tolerance born of indifference, a characteristic of Eastern temperament. Then came the ambitious Calif Abd-er-Rahman by whom the old building was purchased and destroyed, and the building of the great mosque began, on which for an hour a day the Calif himself worked with his own hands."

He completed the first mosque, and his son added the minaret, and the great fountain in the court, hewn out of a block from the Sierra quarries and brought by seventy oxen and one hundred men to its place in the court. For two centuries the mosque grew in size and splendor. The columns and wall were covered with mosaics. Inscriptions from the Koran adorned the entrance gates. New and more splendid minarets were added, and new arcades grew into a forest of columns.

In the eleventh century the Christians regained the site, driving the Moslems from their city. First the pagan Temple, then a Christian Church, then the great

Mosque of Islam, then again a Christian Church which we enter today and feel as Charles V. did when he said to the church dignitaries, "You have built what you or any other could have erected anywhere, but you have destroyed something that was unique in the world."

However, there is enough left for us to feel lost in wonder. We must agree with Mrs. Hartley who says, "There is nothing of the mystic suggestion of the Gothic cathedrals. This Moorish house of prayer brings you a sense of joy, not awe, it frees your spirit, it does not overwhelm." Alas that it was not left as the Moors left it. The detail of the oldest part is a most exquisite example of their genius.

From Cordova the Moors migrated to Toledo, a city also built upon a hill above a river. Narrow, dirty streets crawl upward by stairs to a square at the centre of the city. From it, one enters courts and palaces with terraced gardens leading back to the river.

Georgiana Goddard King, who has written so much of Spain, pictures for us the life in Toledo as it might have been in the eleventh century when it became the royal city. "The little kingdom was free, splendid and learned. The Arabs called it the pearl in the necklace. The streets of the city were steep and pitched down to the Tagus, the banks of which were covered with gardens. Baths were there and pleasure palaces embowered in boscage heavy with the weight of roses and stirred by emulous nightingales. The towered city hung against the blue sky; the call to prayers dropped tinkling through the crystalline air; trumpets sang out, and underneath came the throbbing of a drum beaten outside the palace. In their heavy loose dress, their peaked helmets and linked mail, with weapons carved and inlaid with gold, the tall, brown nobility swung through the narrow ways noiselessly, arrogantly; they brushed past faquies and rabbis and sages, mathematicians, jurists, physicians. The Moslems interfered neither with the Jew or Christian. They allowed them to live easily, worshipping in their own churches where under horseshoe arches the offices of the old rite echo in cadences harsh and unchanging."*

Mrs. Hartley says that one should receive the first impression of Toledo at sunrise from the Puerta del Sol. Then one is transported into the East and the Past. With the Eastern peoples the garden way always led to the Mosques, which one could enter only through a garden. It is hard for us to understand the important part the garden played in the religion of Asiatic people who deified nature and worshipped water, trees, shrubs, and flowers. The Mosque was not the only place for prayer; wherever the Moslem is, at the appointed hour, he brings out his prayer rug and falls on his knees, while the muezzin chants from his minaret that there is no other god but Allah. The minarets give a charming accent to the landscape. They rise beside the domes, tiled in green and gold roofing, every chapel and tomb like so many bubbles in the sunshine.

In Spain, however, in the twelfth century, square towers of brick standing at the corner of the court close to the mosque, took the places of slender minarets. The brick of their surfaces was beautifully overlaid in a weaving design, the lines running diagonally up and down and across the wall, never returning, always turning at an angle and not on a curve, and all the result of careful mathematical planning. At least three of these towers, all built in the twelfth century, and probably

---

*Way of St. James. Georgiana King. Courtesy of G. P. Putnam's Sons.

by one master, Geber of Seville, are still standing,—in Seville, Rabat and Marrakesh.

At a later time the Moors were expelled from city to city until finally they established themselves in Andalusia with Granada as their capital. They loved gardening and the soil of Andalusia was so very fertile that it yielded abundantly under their care. But though some of the Moors were living happily in Andalusia, in other provinces they were having a hard time. Many knew no other home but Spain. They and their fathers had been born there and loved it as their home. When their land was confiscated some took refuge in the abbeys and others even preferred slavery to exile. The Spaniards appreciated their work and were thankful to keep them as artisans. In this way a new style of architecture arose; a combination of Romanesque and Moorish called Mudejar. The square towers described above belong to this period. Hollow tubes of terra cotta, like drainpipes set one on the other, carried interlacing brick arches, and were colored in the Eastern scale of scarlet, green, deep blue and old turquoise. The effect of its richness is indescribable. The filigree plaster walls also belong to this period, an art invented in Damascus. By means of moulds the plaster was so cleverly cast and joined that it had the appearance of being carved, and covers the walls, mellowed with time, as with carved ivory or old lace. With the stalactite ceilings they are unique in the world, and the most striking feature of Arab buildings. Another marked characteristic of Moorish architecture is the use of galleries, called Adarve or Azotea. They run along on the outside of buildings, and the Spaniards, especially the women, love to look down from them on the gay world below, or perhaps to gossip with their neighbors across the narrow street. This is in contrast to the usual Eastern custom of having domestic buildings open into courts, enclosed by walls for safety and seclusion.

A king-poet of Cordova described the difference in the way of life of the Moor from that of the Christian:

"For the poor Christians, the monasteries; for us let us keep the gardens, the harem, the baths and assembly halls rich with jasper and glittering stucco formed of hyacinths, and illuminated by ever-burning lamps. For them the obscure cloisters; for us the fountains of silver and shady orange trees. For them the privations of a fortress life; for us the tranquil and soft existence of our pleasant palaces and smiling haunts. For them intolerant tyranny; for us a mild monarchy. For them the ignorant ambitions of the people; for us the arts. For them, abstinence and martyrdom; but let us enjoy the delights of friendship and of love in the fertile fields of beautiful Andalusia."

We are quite sympathetic with the poet as we look up from the Alameda to the Alhambra, the last stronghold of the Moslems in Spain, and see its red walls rising above the city of Granada. At the close of the fifteenth century, in the heyday of its Oriental glory, it came into the hands of Ferdinand and Isabella. Washington Irving pictures the scene of their entry into possession.

"Up a steep and shady avenue came the royal party to the Gate of Justice where the conquered king, Boabdil, was wont to try his people for petty causes. The great vestibule or porch opens under a huge horseshoe arch, on the outside of which is carved a gigantic hand, and on the inside a gigantic key. To the Moslem the hand symbolized his doctrine, the key his faith; but to the descendants of the exiles the tradition clung that the gate was under the spell of the magician king who built

it, and would stand until the hand grasped the key.*
Coming through the gate, a walk leads up to the esplanade, the Place of the Cisterns, where there is a well of immense depth, furnishing to the Palace an inexhaustible supply of the purest and coldest water. For the grounds and baths, Moorish aqueducts brought water from the distant mountains. The murmur of water overflowing its fountains lingers forever in the memory of those who have wandered in the courts and gardens of this enchanted fortress.

Into the Hall of Justice enter the conquering King and Queen, Ferdinand and Isabella, followed by their triumphant court. Here was celebrated the High Mass. A cross was carved upon the wall, an altar erected, and the Cardinal of Spain officiated, assisted by the highest religious dignitaries of the land. Some say that in the crowd Columbus witnessed the ceremonies.

And what of the unlucky king, Boabdil? Irving claims that "he was personally brave but wanted moral courage, and that his irresolution and feebleness of spirit hastened his downfall and deprived him of that heroic grace which would have rendered it a worthy end to the Moslem domination of Spain." Irving gives us the pathetic story of his request that the gate by which he leaves the Alhambra shall be closed and sealed after him, that he might be the last to pass through it. Through the sympathy of Queen Isabella his request was granted; and no one has passed through it since. It stands in a heap of ruins in an open part of the grounds between the Alhambra and the Generalife. When Boabdil left the palace there was no disfiguring French castle to mar the beauty of the Moorish work. The old red brick walls surrounded the grounds, making a lovely background

---

*The Alhambra. Washington Irving.

for the plum trees and Judas trees blossoming then as now. We enter the Patio de los Arrayanes with its long pool which reflects so exquisitely the myrtle hedge along its sides, the orange trees at the corners, and at either end the loggias with their five arches under filigree walls. It is a favorite place to sit and dream, or read the stories Washington Irving tells of the people who once lived here.

Above the Loggia rises the old fortress tower de Comares, where important personages were imprisoned from time to time. Through the middle arch, from across a dark hall, twin windows frame a charming view of hills and distant snow mountains, and a white mosque standing on a green hill. Crossing the Hall of the Ambassadors you come out on a loggia or gallery and look down on the Patio de Lindaraxa, a curious lopsided enclosure full of tall cypress trees around a lovely lotus-shaped fountain of alabaster. Here the martlet, the only sacred bird in Spain, twitters unmolested, because, so the legend tells, it plucked the thorns off the crown of the crucified Jesus. The garden has romantic charm. According to an Arabic inscription it belonged to the Moorish queens:

"How beauteous is this garden where the flowers of the earth vie with the stars of heaven! What can compare with the vase of yon alabaster fountain filled with crystal water? Nothing but the moon in her fulness, shining in the midst of an unclouded sky."

Near by is the smaller Patio de Reja also full of cypress trees with a dripping fountain in the midst of them. Looking up from the garden the gallery forms a charming background.

Returning to the Patio de los Arrayanes we pass through and enter the Patio de los Leones which has suffered little from the ravages of time. In the center stands a fountain famous in song and story. Here at night are heard mysterious sounds, believed by the credulous to be the revengeful spirits of the Albencerrages wandering through the scene of their suffering. From here one enters the Hall of the Sisters which has a white marble floor and exquisite tiles. The upper part is faced with a fine example of the famous filigree stucco work, embellished with gold, lapis lazuli and other brilliant colors. A stalactite ceiling crowns its glory.

Beyond these courts is a large pool at the entrance to the tiny and perfect mosque of El Partal, which is a little gem, the glory of its coloring unspoiled by time or restoration. Terraced gardens lead from it to a higher level; out of fairy land into the shadow of Charles V.'s monstrous castle.

How impossible to give any idea of the Alhambra! One must see it, and even then can carry away merely an impression of its beauty and romance. "The Alhambra cannot be coldly mirrored in words."

In the outer wall that divides the Alhambra from the Generalife a tower rises where, according to tradition, lived the daughters of the Moorish kings. It is a charming bit of the old palace, and a fitting background for the many romantic tales that cling to its walls. The grounds about it still show traces of what was once an enclosed Moorish garden, full of great box and myrtle trees.

In the old Moorish days a bridge spanned the valley between the Alhambra and the Generalife, the oldest gardens of the Moorish kings. The name is misleading, for it has nothing to do with a general, but means a "lofty garden." It was built in the thirteenth century, and in the fifteenth was given to a Moor who had helped the Catholic king in the conquest of Granada. It is now the property of the Spanish government,—if there is one. It is entered by a long avenue of cypress trees leading to a loggia. From this opens a patio with slender marble columns with a view down a long narrow canal flanked with flowerbeds. Fountains fly high in the air presenting a very charming picture which is repeated by its reflection in the water. A marble colonnade leads into a little mosque, now a chapel. The gardens seem to have grown one from another rather than to have been created all at once. Climbing to the highest terrace of the gardens we rest in the Mirador to enjoy its beautiful view of distant mountains. Then, descending slowly through the terraces we come to fountains and box-bordered flower beds, and the U-shaped water garden belonging to the harem quarter. Near its entrance is a little pool with large plants in pots as the only decoration. Rose Standish Nichols speaks of the Patio de los Cypresses below the water garden as the most enchanting garden she had ever seen. Mrs. Hartley describes it as having a pavement of black and grey river pebbles, a cream-colored wall with green shadows, and green water. There are flower beds of one or two varieties; all a wonderful background for the pink oleander that blooms in June.

The outer wall of the garden is pierced by five open archways dividing the view of the picturesque Albacian hill into panels. In the wall are built seats that tempt one to linger and enjoy them.

To Mrs. Hartley Cordova and Toledo are dead cities, in contrast to Seville, "a living city whose blood is pulsing steadily with the joy of life lived in the sunshine." You feel the difference in walking through the Sevillian streets. Every few steps a big iron gate shows a charming patio behind it, and you feel that this is only the beginning of a series of patios behind the house where the inmates spend their lives in garden rooms. In a little street leading from the Alcazar to the gardens of the Maria Louisa Park, the houses are of creamy white plaster with little balconies from which hang long festoons of luxuriant pink geraniums casting entrancing shadows on the walls. This is the Santa Crux quarter which Waldo D. Frank describes as a "fairy quarter with its rows of ancient houses, a tiny unsuspected court between the blank backs of two houses from which oak doors lead into other courts." Further along the same street is an old house devoted to the memory of Washington Irving and used as a reading room for Americans. At the end of the street a doorway opens into the gardens and house of Murillo, which belongs to the Gothic period. Beyond this is the Maria Louisa Park, a veritable rose garden, where every path and highway is edged with garlands of roses hanging from iron bars in festoons. Apparently there are miles of them. When I saw them in the month of April they were in the perfection of their bloom and no one seemed to think of picking them.

Seville is fortunate in having at least three marked Moorish palaces with characteristic gardens. The house of Pilatus is built around an atrium through which glimpses of the Oriental garden beyond make one long for an invitation to enter, a longing rarely satisfied. The gardens of the Palacio de los Duenas are open to the public, and still retain their Moorish charm. There are many patios, each with its fountain and marble columns shaded by tall palm trees which give a tropical accent. The gardens of the Alcazar are the most interesting in Seville. The most ancient part of the palace is Moorish. Pedro the Cruel lived here and here he brought his bride,

Blanche of Castile, only to leave her three days later for his mistress, Maria de Padilla. Maria was indulged in all her whims. Seeing some children wading in the mud outside the palace she decided to do the same thing, so one of the courtyards was strewn with rare perfumes and moistened to the condition of glorified slush, and she and her companions amused themselves in it for a short time.

With the help of Moorish workmen Pedro began his gardens in the Mudejar style. The Alcazar is an excellent example of Oriental Arabian architecture. Beneath it are the ruins of the Sultan's castle which covered a much greater area; reaching with its garden the Golden Tower, one of the fortresses on the Guadalquivir. Moorish workmen in rebuilding used the Arabic materials and plan. The Patio de las Doncellas opens out of the larger court. In it stand pots of flowers. South of the buildings extend the large gardens added to by Charles V., whose little pavilion is a charming spot. I spent hours in the Alcazar wandering up and down tile steps, resting on tiled seats around tiled fountains, and revelling in the roses. I wished I could read the Arabic descriptions in decorative lettering around the gates and patios. Everywhere there are shadows: in the water, on the wall and on the pavements.

The builders of the Moorish gardens in Spain had for their models the gardens of Persia and Syria. The Mongolians after their invasion of Persia carried the art of gardening as they found it there to India. So the gardens of Moorish Spain and the Taj-Mahal have a common ancestry.

When the Moors were expelled from Spain, they took refuge in North Africa, where their ancestors had established themselves centuries before. Naturally the exiled Moors found there a congenial atmosphere, and today we can step back into the fifteenth century gardens and find the life of the fifteenth century still going on in the fascinating cities of Tenes, Meknes, Rabat, Fez, and Marrakesh.

Though the poet-king quoted above scorned the Christian mode of life, the Benedictines and the Cistercians continued to establish their abbeys and monasteries in Spain, carrying on the cultivation of their gardens and the copying of manuscripts. With them the exiled Moors took refuge, enjoying the peace of their protected lives. The lonely abbey was not wholly cut off from the great world outside. Many of the abbots were correspondents of the brilliant Desiderius of Monte Casino and held intercourse with Rome and Byzantium.

The Abbey of Huelgas near Burgos was particularly important. The Abbess was a most imposing person, ruling over her lands, and teaching and controling her nuns, who all belonged to the nobility. The grounds of the Abbey are still very beautiful and it is still a refuge for noblewomen.

Though our garden way lies in Moorish Spain, we cannot leave the country without remembering Charles V., who, weary of Empire building, abdicated and retired to the peace of monastic life. He was a great lover of gardens and intensely interested in botany. When he retired, a sick old man, into the monastery of San Jeronimo at San Juste, he devoted his time to mechanical amusements and to gardening. He built for himself a building adjoining the monastery, where from his bedroom he could participate in the celebration of the mass through an open door. From his workroom he looked down on his unfinished garden where he had himself worked, and from which there was a wonderful view of the hills. It was planted with orange and lemon trees, with citron and sweet-smelling herbs. From botanists of the time he obtained plants that grew in every part of his kingdom. He delighted in color and perfume, and in his last illness his garden and the cloistered farm were still a pleasure to him, though he could no longer till the ground or cull his roses, or even visit the Stations of the Cross which he had placed in his garden.

CHAPTER VII

A PATH OF ADVENTURE

"Spanish America is the principal monument
to the greatness of Charles I.'s reign—"

WASHINGTON IRVING

CHAPTER VII

On the coast of Andalusia there is still standing a small and unassuming Franciscan convent, dedicated to Santa Maria de Rabida. Near by is the little harbor of Palos, a seaport town inhabited by sea-faring men, the adventurous spirits of the fifteenth century.

It is the fifteenth of March in the year 1493, and Prior Juan Perez comes forth from the convent and finds the porter on the bluff gazing intently out to sea. The Prior joins him, and he too looks out to the horizon where he can just see a ship under full sail coming towards the harbor. It isn't a fishing boat. Even at a distance they see that. Both men are sea-wise. The porter turns to the Prior and in an awestruck voice asks what he thinks it is. Juan Perez, a man of extensive information in nautical affairs wonders if it can be the Santa Maria. The porter says, "No, it looks more like the Nina to me." As they watch the little boat slowly sailing in, they recall the day when Christopher Columbus came as a stranger to the convent asking bread for his little boy. The Prior was so impressed by him that he carried the story to the Queen, with whom, as her confessor, he had considerable influence. Isabella took his advice, and espousing the cause of Columbus, fitted him out with a fleet.

The two men now watched the approach of the boat. The porter sighed, "It is not the Santa Maria. It stands in the water more like the Nina." The Prior remembered that the Porter's son went with Columbus on the Santa Maria. How terrible those days were when the little town of Palos was full of sorrowing mothers and doubting Thomases. "Crazy, simply crazy, what good would that little compass of Roger Bacon's do in unknown seas?" However, enough crazy adventurers were tempted, or forced to go. For nearly a year not one word had come from the fleet and now here in the harbor one of the little boats was back; and yes, there was the admiral waving to the crowd, which, by this time, had heard the news and rushed to the harbor. They fell to and helped the admiral unload. With him came "Indians" different from any human beings they had ever seen. Quantities of gay parrots were brought out; new trees and shrubs followed.

Columbus told the people of the wonderful trees all over the islands he had come from. He said that in October the country there was as fresh and green as in the month of May in Andalusia. Not only the trees but the fruits, the herbs, the flowers, the very stones for the most part, were as different from those of Spain as night from day. He was sure he had reached the country described by Marco Polo, where the singing of birds was such that it seemed as if one would never wish to depart. The flocks of parrots there obscured the sun and there were many kinds of birds, large and small, all different from those known in Spain. "And besides these," he went on to say, "there are thousands of species of trees, each having its particular fruit, and of such marvellous flavor I was in the greatest trouble in the world not to know them, for I am very certain they are of great value. I have brought home some as specimens and also some of the herbs. I am sure that these come from the islands of India that Marco Polo told about in his wonderful book. The air was full of the scent of spices." He thought they would be of much value for tinctures, medicines and spices, and was eager to find out about them in the great book of Albertus Magnus. All of which he wrote immediately in a letter to their majesties of Spain. Before long he was on the ocean again, this time with a large fleet equipped without any trouble. Everyone was eager to brave the dangers in order to gather the gold of which the land was supposed to have untold wealth. Columbus was fortunate in having a sympathetic friend in Peter Martyr, to whom he wrote freely. Peter Martyr was the authorized historian for Isabella and from his "Decades" Washington Irving drew much material for his story of the discovery of America.

The subject of gardens was apparently of very little interest in those days, though Columbus was much impressed by the natural wonders of the new world. On his second voyage he cruised among innumerable islands and spent a day running along the coast of one that the Indians called Boriquen (now Porto Rico). At the west end Columbus discovered an excellent harbor. Landing he found a road which led to a village not far away, the first one of any account he had seen.

"It was built around a common square, like a market place, with large and well built houses. The road had fences on each side made of interwoven reeds, inclosing fruitful gardens. At the end of the road was a kind of terrace or lookout constructed of reeds and overhanging the water. The whole place had an air of neatness and ingenuity and appeared to be the abode of some important chieftain."*

A companion of Columbus, Ponce de Leon, landed here, and found himself near the house of the Cacique, Aquebana. Friendly relations were immediately established and names exchanged. Among the Indians this was the pledge of perpetual amity. Ponce de Leon visited the Cacique and met his family which consisted of

*Life of Columbus. Washington Irving.

his mother, his stepfather, brother and sister. He was then shown over the island by the Cacique, who pointed out his productive fields of yucca, from which the cassava bread was made. The purest spring of water was shown and he was told of river beds full of pebbles richly veined with gold.

The first Christian settlement in the new world was on the island of Hayti, where the Spaniards found a favorable site for a city with a good harbor and place for a fortress. The climate was excellent, the soil fertile and two rivers filled with fish united there. The place was laid out according to a plan with streets and squares, a church, a public storehouse and a residence for the admiral built of stone; ... the other houses were of wood, plaster or reeds. The city was enclosed with walls and named Isabella in honor of the Queen. In it Columbus planted a garden with seeds brought from Spain, and outside the walls large fields of sugar cane.

After a two months expedition into the mountains for gold, he returned and found his garden flourishing. Seeds had become plants, sugar cane had increased. A native vine had responded favorably to cultivation; cuttings sent from home had already begun to form clusters. Ears of corn were served to Columbus in March, the seeds of which were planted in January. Garden herbs came to maturity in sixteen days, and melons, gourds, and cucumbers were ready for the table within a month of seed planting. It is a pity the garden-loving monks had not come with Columbus to these islands. Though he made three more voyages, I find no further record of garden-making.

The discovery of the Pacific was left to Vasco Nuñez de Balboa, who first heard of it on one of his expeditions into the interior. Pointing to the western mountains the Indians told him that if gold was what he sought he had only to cross these to find a great sea into which flowed rivers of gold. The kings there ate from golden bowls and used it as the Spaniards used iron. This was the first news of a Western sea that came to the invaders. Naturally Balboa became absorbed in plans for reaching it. The story is a thrilling one. Finally the difficulties were overcome and Balboa on St. Michael's Day, 1513, looking down on the ocean, from the summit of a mountain, took possession of the land and sea. Then, after a perilous descent to the shore he unfurled a banner on which was a picture of the Virgin and Child, and proclaimed in the name of the monarchs of Castile, Leon and Aragon, the possession of the seas, and lands, coasts, ports, and islands for all time. Nobody disputing his right, thanks to God were offered and three crosses, symbolic of the Trinity, were cut on the trees.

In the same year Ponce de Leon planted the cross in Florida. He had come to America with a Royal permit to govern the island of Boriquen, and was married to a very young Spanish girl whose father had died in his arms, leaving the daughter in his care. Ponce had been her protector ever since and in addition had fallen in love with her, a passion which she returned. It was a great trial to him to be so much older than his young bride; hearing of a miracle fountain where all who drank of it three times had a renewal of youth, he decided to go in search of it. An old Indian told him that the fountain was on the island across the water. The young bride begged him not to leave her. She would rather have him remain and enjoy the beautiful home he had built. But the promise of youth was too great a temptation. He equipped two boats and took the old Indian woman, who had told him of the fountain, as guide, and off they went, leaving the young wife in charge of their home.

On the twenty-seventh of March he came in sight of the coast of Florida, which he supposed to be the island he was in search of. On the second of April, Easter Sunday, he landed and named the land Florida in honor of the Pasqua Florida. With him, as usual on these expeditions, were a number of priests, who conducted according to custom, the service of occupation. It began with the following prayer:

"Oh Lord Almighty and everlasting God, by Thy holy word Thou hast created the heavens, the earth and the sea. May Thy name be blessed and glorified; praised be Thy majesty, oh Thou who through Thy humble servant hast ordained that Thy sacred name shall be made known and proclaimed in these new regions of the world. May the blessing of Almighty God, Son and Holy Ghost descend and abide for ever."

Following the prayer a cross was planted by laying fifteen stones East and West and thirteen North and South forming a cross, commemorating the year 1513. Today it is shown in the little garden around the Fountain of Youth, the fountain that Ponce de Leon never found.

In Mexico City, discovered by Cortez in 1519, the natives were very superior to those encountered on the islands. Perhaps the most civilized of them were the Tolbecs who occupied the great table land. They belonged to the Maya group and probably were descended from an earlier civilization than the Maya or Pyramid builders, whose stone carving showed such a high degree of civilization. All these tribes were agricultural, cultivating the mountain sides by means of terraces. They lived in large, well built towns and with an efficient form of government. Their houses were large, and many of them were decorated with carved stone work. The industries of the towns were weaving, pottery, gold and silver work. At the time of Cortez's invasion the Indian chief was Montezuma, of the Aztec tribe, really an emperor, with great power, who hated and feared the Spaniards. To propitiate them he sent presents to Cortez and tried to persuade him not to come to Tenoctititland, (Mexico City), but Cortez was not to be turned aside from his quest. He was received by Montezuma with courtesy which he returned by making him a prisoner in his own house, a very splendid palace with a hundred rooms built around three open squares of such extent that one invader recorded that "he wandered around four times until he was tired, and yet did not see the whole."

Another Aztec chief had an equally interesting palace, and this time we are told that the palace stood in the midst of groves and pleasure gardens. Stone steps and terraces still bear witness to the truth of the chronicler. In the gardens there were rare flowers, transplanted from warm countries with religious ceremony. All kinds of birds and beasts were kept in well appointed zoological gardens where there were homes for alligators and snakes.

The Aztecs worshipped a sun god, but beyond this they had an invisible god who had no image and was propitiated, not by bloody sacrifices but by flowers and incense. They believed that one god came into the land to teach men to till the soil and to work in metals. With the sun god they associated a moon goddess. Their temple was called god's house and rivaled in size the temples of Babylon. It was built on a mount on a square or oblong base, rising in terraces to a small platform on the top. A large proportion of the inhabitants were set apart for the priesthood, and festivals were frequent.

The Aztecs knew the value of wood ashes in agriculture. The chroniclers tell that they burned bushes and trees and in the ashes planted their seeds. From Mexico the Spaniards learned the use of chocolate, tomato, and chili. The Mexicans wore clothes of woven aloe and palm fibre. Cotton was used extensively. It was often woven in fine texture and embroidered in color. Everything suggested wealth.

When one looks at the map, the East doesn't seem so very far away from Mexico, and one can readily believe that these historic people may have drifted over the sea from China or India and some learned people believe that the continents were either nearer together or that another continent lay between them in prehistoric times.

In 1532 De Soto entered Peru, the country of the Incas. Here the cities were enclosed in great walls of huge blocks of stones as carefully laid as the walls of China. A magnificent highway far superior to any in Spain led to the capitol which the natives burned rather than let it fall into the hands of the Spaniards. Scholars tell us that the rudiments of the arts, of agriculture, of pottery making, of weaving and of metallurgy existed along the Peruvian coast and highlands at a remote period. A collection of weaving in the Boston Art Museum is extremely interesting and shows a similarity to Chinese art. One poncho has a real Chinese red background on which squat sun gods, looking very Chinese.

On one of the hills, Tiahuanaco, remains of a temple to the sun god have been found. Apparently it stood in a grove similar to the temples of the East. Over the gate is a carving in stone of the sun god wearing a shirt with long sleeves and a belt with human heads carved in a more or less conventional manner. Around the head of the god an aureole of sun's rays suggests Ahknaton's sun's rays.

Their myth of creation is unique: A deluge laid waste the land leaving only one man and one woman, carried by the wind to Lake Tiahuanaco, where the Creator began to raise up people and nations, making one of each nation, of clay, and painting the dresses that each one was to wear. Those that were to wear their hair, with hair, and those that were to be shorn, with hair cut. The images were then distributed upon the earth and imbued with life.

One of the high lights of De Soto's expedition in Florida was an incident on the banks of the Savannah where the Indian village of Copachiqui stood. De Soto was met by a highly decorated canoe, in which was a gorgeous palanquin, borne by four men. From it descended a showily dressed girl with eight girl attendants. Several other canoes followed and six ambassadors headed the procession. As the young Princess stepped from the canoe the Spaniards were deeply impressed by her dignity, grace and beauty. They thought her as perfect as a Greek statue. Her attendants brought with them a chair of state upon which she seated herself after bowing courteously to De Soto. Taking from her neck a string of pearls she placed them around his neck to show her favor and to gain his good will. She also presented him with blankets and skins, dried venison and wafers, and an abundance of good salt. All the Indians were clothed down to their feet in fine skins and hand woven blankets. The skins were of sable and wildcat, which gave out a strong smell. Their leggings were made of black leather laced with white and topped with fringes of colored leather. The men wore queer head-dresses and carried shields of hide, and the women were dressed in white cloth, hand woven of very fine fibre from the mulberry trees. The Princess ordered rafts made to transport the Spaniards to the village and offered half of her own residence to De Soto for his accommodation; and half the wigwams in the village for his soldiers. These are described as commodious and agreeably situated in a mulberry grove.

The house of the Princess was large and decorated inside with handsome mats arranged so skillfully they appeared to be one. About the house wild strawberries were growing, which were much appreciated by the visitors—and wild roses were spoken of as being very fragrant.

The mother of the Princess was a widow living about thirty miles down the river and De Soto, eager to make friends with the tribe, asked to see her. The Princess sent her chieftains to persuade her to come and meet the strangers, but she refused and said she highly disapproved of her daughter's conduct as inexpedient and indelicate.

When the time came for departure, the Princess was obliged to guide the Spaniards through her kingdom practically as a prisoner. As the borderland came near, she slipped into the forest and escaped from her captors.

The journey to the Mississippi was long and perilous and very disappointing to all who sought gold. At last another cross was planted on the bank above the river with imposing ceremony. And shortly after this the beloved leader died and was buried in the river. The remnant of the great expedition struggled on to Mexico, then the stronghold of the Spaniards, who named the country New Spain.

There was living in Mexico at this time the friar Emanuel de Villegas who had found in Peru a flower of great beauty that he called the Passion Flower. Hearing that the historian of the Knights of Malta, Bosio, was writing his great work, "The Cross Triumphant," he sent to him a description of this flower. The description was so extraordinary that Bosio hesitated to use it, until other travelers corroborated the story. The story of the plant created a great excitement among the botanists and theologians of the day, and led to its introduction soon after into both Spain and Italy where it became the beautiful symbol of Christ's passion. It is still used as a favorite design for ecclesiastical decoration and is America's contribution to the wreath of symbolic flowers.

The whole story of the Spanish expeditions comes to us through the journals of the priests. Throughout the sixteenth and seventeenth centuries they devoted themselves to the work of bringing the native tribes into the Christian church. The Jesuits, the first to come, were untiring in their efforts. Propitiating the natives with presents they soon learned the influence of music over them. The Roman Catholic Ritual was pleasing to them and in various ceremonies of occupation they joined in the service.

The Spaniards in Mexico sent the missionaries off to explore the country and make ready for its conquest. In this way they forced their way into New Mexico, establishing missions as far north as Santa Fe.

In the May, 1933, number of "Travel" there is a delightful article on the "Garden Cities of Old Mexico," in which the author, Mr. James P. Jenkins, tells us that there are still in Mexico cities with houses and gardens begun in the sixteenth century. There life goes on today as it did four hundred years ago. Mr. Jenkins tells us of the hill town of Uruapan, the name of which means "the gourd where flowers are blooming." This hill is shaped like a gourd upside down and though the altitude is over five thousand feet, the climate is almost too balmy. In the city the houses are built around patios, each one a luxuriant garden. Outside the city proper are detached houses surrounded by gardens in which the families appear to spend their lives happily and easily. Every family raises its own eggs, coffee and fruit at its doors. Their fruits are noted for their size, sweetness, color and aroma. The gardens are surrounded with stone walls over which climb luxuriant vines. Passion flowers, planted in oil cans, reach to the thatched roofs where orchids bloom. Family wash hangs over tea roses and every imaginable flower blooms in the walled-in gardens, while gay tropical birds give an added flash of color against a background of snow covered peaks.

The name Uruapan has another interesting significance derived from the art-craft of lacquer bowls for which the place was famous when the Spaniards first came. These bowls and trays were taken back to Spain as souvenirs by the Conquistadores in the days of Charles V. They were decorated with gay floral designs with black background, highly glazed and very similar to the famous Chinese lacquer. Mr. Jenkins considers them another link in the chain connecting our Western lands with China. An unproven theory is that the art was introduced in 600 by Chinese rovers who taught the technique to the Mayan race of Indians.

The Spaniards settled in Mexico which they called New Spain and had they had the training and experience in self government that the English had had they might have established a great empire in the West and our country might have been more Spanish than English. Fortunately for us the latter were industrious and patient colonizers and not quite so sanguine as the Spaniard in the expectation of finding gold to be had for the asking. Englishmen, impoverished by incessant warfare, sought to replenish their purses in the new land which, according to rumor, abounded in undeveloped wealth. However, it was the Spanish adventurer that found our country and blazed the trail which the English soon followed. "Wherever the Spanish or Portuguese conquistadores occupied fresh territories in the new world, they were followed by Jesuit fathers. If unknown regions were to be explored, it was the Jesuits who volunteered to undertake the task; when peace treaties or alliances were to be concluded with the Indians the authorities made use of the fathers, for they alone were acquainted with the native dialects, and on account of their constant friendliness, enjoyed the full confidence of the chieftains."*

In Mexico the Jesuits were the first to venture among the northern tribes. "With Mexico as their base of operations, they pushed forward into New Mexico, Arizona, California and Texas."* They were also untiring in their work of colonization in South America. The Mission of San Xavier near Tucson in Arizona was established by them, and is the only one that has never ceased to carry on its noble work for the uplift of the Indians. For two hundred years and more, services have been held on Sunday mornings in the grand old church. Indians of all ages still come, grandfathers in their old-time blankets and moccasins, granddaughters in cheap machine-made garments, and high-heeled shoes. Their children walk ten miles a day to attend school.

In the seventeenth century almost simultaneously with the English, the French landed on the east coast of North America and founded New France, now Canada.

---

*The Power and Secret of the Jesuits. Fulop-Miller. Courtesy of Viking Press.

Jesuit priests came with them and one of the first buildings of the new settlement of Quebec was the Jesuit college. Bancroft writes that: "the origin of all towns in French America is closely associated with the work of missionaries; not a cape was rounded, not a river discovered without a Jesuit's having shown the way."

Father Marquette and Louis Joliet became the first Europeans after De Soto to reach that legendary stream of which the Indian had so often spoken. In their boats they came to New Orleans, out of which they drove the Spaniards; their descendants claim as French work the open squares, the tiny patios, filled with potted plants, and the characteristic Spanish wrought iron balconies.

In 1649, the year in which Charles I. was beheaded, there appeared in England a most alluring pamphlet extolling the possibilities of the new world where "already there are fifty thousand English people with three hundred negro servants." Many domesticated animals and innumerable wild ones were to be had for the taking. Excellent fish were in the rivers, and wild turkeys weighing sixty pounds overran the country. It also tells of the song birds, and mentions particularly the "mock bird" and the "gay rare colored paraketoes." The farmers had under cultivation many hundred acres of wheat and Virginia corn; fruit that rivaled that of Italy; and in the gardens grew potatoes, turnips, carrots, parsnips, onions, artichokes, asparagus, beans and better peas than those of England, with all manner of herbs and 'physick flowers'. Such quantities of tobacco were raised that it sold for only three pence the pound. "There is also a hope that indigo, hemp and flax vines and silk worms could be cultivated with profit, since it is chiefly hands that are wanted."

"At the same time they are hoping soon to discover

a way to China, for Sir Francis Drake was on the back side of Virginia in his voyage about the world in 37 degrees, and now all the question is how broad the land may be to that place from the head of James River above the falls."

It goes on to say that "New England is only four days sail from Virginia," and from there a trade goes to and fro, but except for the fishing "there is not much in that." What a pity that the New England people "being now about twenty thousand did not seat themselves at first to the south of Virginia, in a warm and rich country, where their industry would have produced sugar, indigo, ginger, cotton and the like commodities."

Naturally a pamphlet of this nature fed the imagination of discontented royalists in England. Then too by this time the Protectorate was closing monasteries and taking over the great estates, belonging to Royalty and nobility, to turn them into vegetable gardens. There was much indignation and unhappiness in old England, and it was not surprising that the pamphlet called "A Perfect Description of Virginia," in which readers are told that there is nothing wanting to make people happy in that new land should have packed the boats with immigrants, rich and poor.

The commerce between Virginia and the north, of which the Englishman spoke so lightly, rapidly developed the seaport towns of New England, especially Salem and Portsmouth, from whence ships sailed in the wake of Drake and Magellan, bringing prosperity to the sturdy pioneers on the rock-bound coast of the north. Here the little dooryard gardens enclosed in picket fences were filled with old time favorites immortalized by Shakespeare; the women folks brought with them seeds and treasured cuttings across the sea and raised their herbs and hardy vegetables, learning to concoct their household remedies with the help of the friendly Indian. Ships returning from the east brought many an eastern treasure to brighten the dooryards. The peony, the azalea, the wistaria, the lilacs, the roses, what would New England be without them!

The villages were built around a spacious common at the head of which stood the meeting house, the social center, but here life was austere and hard. Problems were brought to the meeting house and laid before God in prayer. Upright and brave were the pioneers. Their faith was strong. We wish there had been a little more love mixed with the faith—love that could have spared the witches and buried the little unbaptized babies in consecrated ground.

As prosperity came, the little meeting houses grew into noble buildings. Our New England ancestors had a fine sense of proportion. Bullfinch brought from England Sir Christopher Wren's ideas, whose charming white spires still point to the sky in New England villages, and the interiors carry English decorative designs.

With the dawn of the eighteenth century the Atlantic coast line had become a veritable stretch of old England. Through Virginia, which then meant the whole coast, great tidal rivers ran. On these the plantations were established. Here the garden way was a waterway. Ships came to the landings bringing furniture and many kinds of trees, shrubs and plants for the new homes, and went back to England loaded with rice and tobacco. Boys went too, to be educated in Oxford and Cambridge.

The interchange of plant life was of absorbing interests, the botanists of both continents vying with each other in the acclimating of native flora. In addition to the pine, the fir, the hemlock, the maple, the oak, and the rarer tulip tree, the live-oak, the catalpa, the magnolia and rhododendron migrated, some from England and others from the East. Boxwood and ivy were especially popular and extensively used in the South.

There the center of the social life was the little English church surrounded with trees. Its devoted sons and daughters came to the services in canoes before the first road was laid out, which we are told, led to the church of St. Andrews, in the midst of plantations not far from Charleston. This little church, surrounded with saddle horses and gay ladies, was a favorite subject for the artist. The gay ladies came in chaises, the acme of luxury. The clothes they wore, and all manufactured household goods, came from Europe. Silks and satins found their way across the sea for the Colonial girls, one of whom, Eliza Lucas, wrote delightful letters to a friend in England, giving vivid pictures of her life in the new world. She was sixteen years old and to her had been given the care of several plantations, where she raised rice and tobacco and experimented in indigo. Her father was governor of one of the islands settled by Columbus, the climate of which did not agree with his wife. Consequently she and Eliza were settled on the Ashley River, a very select colony.

She tells of a tour arranged to show her "those parts of the country in which are several very handsome gentlemen's seats at which they were entertained with the most friendly politeness. The first we arrived at was Crowfield where we spent a most agreeable week. The house stands a mile from the road and makes a very handsome appearance. As you draw nearer, new beauties discover themselves; first the beautiful vine mantling the wall, laden with delicious clusters. Next a large pond, in the midst of a spacious green, presents itself as you enter the gate. From the back door is a wide walk a thousand feet long, each side of which nearest to the house is a grass plot, ornamented in a serpentine manner with flowers; next to that on the right hand is what immediately struck my rural taste, a thicket of tall young live oaks, where a variety of airy choristers poured forth their melody, and, my darling,—the mocking bird, joined in the concert, enchanting me with his harmony.

"Opposite on the left bank is a large bowling green, sunk a little below the rest of the garden, with a walk quite round, bordered by a double row of fine large flowering Laurel and Catalpas, which afford both shade and beauty. My letter will be of unseasonable length if I do not pass over the Mounts, wilderness, etc., and come to the boundary of this charming spot where is a large fish pond with a Mount rising out of the middle, the top of which is level with the dwelling house and upon it is a Roman Temple. On each side are other large fish ponds properly disposed which form a fine prospect of water from the house. Beyond are the smiling fields dressed in vivid green."

In another letter she describes her own home: "I have a little library in which I spend part of my time. My music and my garden, which I am very fond of, take up the rest that is not employed in business, of which my father has left me a pretty good share! Which indeed was unavoidable as my mamma's bad state of health prevents her going through any fatigue. I have the business of three plantations to transact, which requires much writing and more business and fatigue of other sorts than you can imagine. But lest you should imagine it to be hard to a girl at my early time of life, give me leave to assure you that I consider myself happy that I can be useful to so good a father."*

Every time a boat came from England, some one brought a book. The "Spectator" was eagerly read, and we can picture Eliza in her library absorbed in some new article on agriculture. At this time the burning question was the use of artificial architecture in gardens— the clipping of trees to imitate stone in walls and statues was emphatically condemned by Lord Shaftsbury. Addison published in the "Spectator" an essay explaining the difference between open wild nature and art in the garden. He was a traveled gentleman, familiar with French and Italian gardens, and much taken with the latter, but closes his essay in praise of natural trees in bloom. Pope with his wit and satire helped the revolt declaring that artists love nature unadorned, and regard art as nothing more than an imitation of nature.

The first landscape gardener in America that we have record of was a Frenchman and imported to lay out a vast estate on the Ashley for Lord Middleton, probably the one described by Eliza Lucas. It still belongs to the Middleton family and can be visited today. Visitors are allowed to wander at will and enjoy its beauty. For ten years the landscape gardener directed one hundred slaves in the creation of formal terraces, walks, and ornamental waters, skillfully blending the glory of the coastal forests, the wistful vistas of river and marsh, with the well-ordered beauty of the English garden. Not far away lie the magnolia gardens as old as the Middleton estate. Here nature has adorned herself. There is very little formality apparent. A pond reflects in its black water the brilliant colors of azalea, now grown to

---

*Letters of Eliza Lucas Pinckney. Harriott Horry Ravenal. Courtesy of Charles Scribner's Sons.

great trees. Spanish moss hangs in long veils from the trees, a path winds in and out, the birds sing, dreams and fancies come and go.

The James River vied with the Ashley and Tidewater-Virginia had many famous estates, very English in character. The houses were mostly built of brick made on the place, with gardens enclosed where parterres, box bordered, were filled with flowers, old time favorites, and herbs in "knotted" beds; and vegetables with orchards beyond; lawns, a recent development in England, were dotted with splendid specimen trees and stretched to the river banks. Often the box grew into trees supplying the place in America of the ilex trees of Italy. Crepe myrtle was also extensively used and the whole region became famous for its beautiful homes, most of which were built about 1730.

The Marquis de Chastellux visiting Monticello in 1782 said that "we may safely aver that Mr. Jefferson is the first American who has consulted the fine arts to know how he should shelter himself from the weather." While there were many stately mansions built before Jefferson's buildings, they were built after English pattern and in simpler form. Jefferson's houses had porticoes after the Greek fashion in temples. While Jefferson is often called the father of American democracy, he also created a style of architecture aristocratic and classic. His buildings, set in gardens and parks, remind one of the Greek temples set in groves. Monticello, built by Jefferson, of brick made on the place, is approached by winding roadways climbing the hill on which the house stands. The outlook from the house commands an extensive view of the Blue Ridge Mountains and the rolling country of Piedmont, Virginia. Many of the trees and shrubs Jefferson planted with his own hands.

The Campus at the University of Virginia is his masterpiece. The buildings surrounding it are on a rise of ground to which a serpentine road with "secret gardens" leads to its peace and quiet.

For nearly a hundred years Mount Vernon had been the home of the Washingtons. The first of the family to throw in their lot with the new country were Col. John Washington, who came over in 1657, with his brother Lawrence. Staunch royalists, they regarded themselves as still living in an English colony. Unfair taxation, however, was the burning question of the day even then.

George Washington was their great grandson, born in 1731. His half-brother Lawrence gave him work at Mount Vernon as a surveyor. There he met Lord Fairfax, who took a great fancy to him and appointed him surveyor of his back lands. A trip to the Barbadoes with his brother, and a perilous journey to the Ohio to negotiate with Indians, gave him the training needed for his career of responsibility.

In 1759 he writes in his journal from Mount Vernon, "I am now, I believe, fixed at this seat with an agreeable consort for life, and hope to find more happiness in retirement than I ever experienced amidst a wide and bustling world." For six years he lived the life of a farmer, breeding his cattle and making a reputation for his "George Washington" flour, passed without inspection in England because his reputation for honest goods had crossed the sea. Entries in his diary show his love, and habit, of early rising to visit the plantations. He tried making a plow after his own invention, but did not succeed very well. He looked after his negroes and kept every one busy. His experiment of plowing in buckwheat twice a year for fertilizer, and the trying out of different seeds show his flair for detail.

After six years on his farm, the war broke out. At its close he returned to Mount Vernon to find his buildings "Suffering from many wounds." To keep himself out of debt he is obliged to sell lands. In 1789 a deputation from Congress waited on him at Mount Vernon and announced that he was unanimously elected President of the United States. To his intimate friend, Gen. Knox, he writes: "In confidence I tell you that my movement to the chair of government will be accompanied by feelings not unlike those of a culprit who is going to the place of his execution."* At the close of his administration he came back to his beloved "vine and fig tree" and had three happy years there.

The place is beautifully preserved by the "Ladies of the Mount Vernon Association"; every state in the Union has a representative, and every citizen takes pride in it. There one wanders in the box bordered gardens where Dame Martha picked her old-time flowers and berries or into the little cottages where she taught her slaves their household duties.

The new government had its headquarters in Philadelphia, then a little Dutch town laid out on spacious lines, where each householder was enjoined to place his building in the center of a plot that he might be surrounded by verdure. In such a garden home lived John Bartram, the first great botanist of our country. Here Washington was a frequent visitor, and Benjamin Franklin experimented with his host in the mysteries of hybridizing. Here was organized the "Philadelphia Society for promoting agriculture." One wonders if Bartram was the first to import tulips from Holland.

In 1800 the headquarters of the government moved to Washington, then the center of the country. It was

---
*Seven Ages of Washington. Owen Wister. Courtesy of Macmillan Co.

a poor little village. Washington never lived in the White House. President Adams was its first official occupant and moved in before it was finished. Gossip tells us that Mrs. Adams used the East Room as a laundry. Even when Madison moved in, in 1809, he found the town without light or police, with muddy streets and few sidewalks.

Fortunately the statesmen of that day had far-seeing eyes and employed, on the advice of Washington, the French architect L'Enfant to draw up a plan for the city. On paper it resembles a great kite, and in reality it has worked out into a veritable garden city in which every American can justly take pride.

Meanwhile in the Franciscan convent at Palma on the island of Majorca in 1731 a follower of St. Francis enters the order and takes the name of Junipero out of love for the jovial and pure-hearted companion of St. Francis. Filled with eagerness for service, young and brilliant as a preacher, he asks to be sent on a mission and with four college companions joins a band of missionaries gathering at Cadiz to go to Mexico. It took them ninety-nine days to sail from Cadiz to Vera Cruz. From there he and Palou, one of his college companions, asked permission to be allowed to walk to the City of Mexico, a hundred leagues away.

On New Year's day 1750 Junipero Serra entered the college of San Fernando in Mexico City and for seventeen years carried on a devoted life of missionary work in Mexico. He was chosen to take charge of the organization of the missions of Old California, and his devoted friend Palou was given the official care of them. From this time on Serra's life in California is largely the record of its early history, faithfully recorded by Palou. Coronado had long before this reached Lower California and penetrated into New Mexico, where the Jesuits had established themselves. Following or leading, as the case may be, the Jesuits came with the French down the Mississippi. For some political reasons they were expelled from California, and the Franciscans under Padre Serra and his companion Palou were put in charge of Lower California. According to the custom of the Spaniards the expense was defrayed by the crown and the priests were escorted by the civil authority.

In establishing their settlements the civil, religious, and military forces were involved. A civil settlement was called the pueblo, a corporate town. The mission was the religious establishment under the control of the laws but directed by the Padre Presidente in this case Junipero Serra. The ultimate expectation of the King in establishing the missions was that, as soon as the Indians were Christianized, civilized and self-supporting, the missions would become civil pueblos and parish churches. Both pueblo and mission were guarded by the Presidio or fortress. Chapels were to be established as branches of the Missions where there were ranches at a distance from the main settlement. Such was the plan to be followed, worked out by Galvez and Serra.

Their orders were to occupy and fortify San Diego and Monterey, for God and the King of Spain. Two boats were equipped with carpenters, tools and supplies and sent off in fine style, but the padres asked permission to go by land. It was a long trail over untrodden hills covered with brush, but the padres carried on in spite of hardship and disappointment; and finally arrived at San Diego soon after the arrival of one of the boats, the other unfortunately was lost. "With a courage sublime in its boldness, this handful of priests grappled with their task, and brought the vast horde of untamed Indians under subjection, trained them to systematic work, and in a few short years so thoroughly accomplished what they had determined, that the mission buildings were erected by these former savages."*

After establishing the Mission at San Diego in 1769, Monterey was built. San Bonaventura, San Gabriel, San Luis Obispo, San Juan Capistrano followed, and finally San Francisco was reached. The foundation of the Presidio was laid on Sept. 17, 1775. On St. Francis Day, Oct. 9, 1775, the dedication of the mission took place. High mass was celebrated by Padre Serra in the presence of his friend and companion, Palou, and the Mission received its formal name of San Francisco.

One wonders if Padre Serra ever heard of the American Revolution. It would not have interested him very much. To him California was part of Mexico from whence he brought the plans for his missions. The architectural plan was not Moorish Spanish but Romanesque, with splendid wide arches and great spaces of plaster walls. In several cases the doorways carry out the plasteresque style of decoration with Aztec design. Some of the wall spaces were ornamented with plaster panels, a rather crude copy, probably from memory, of the silversmith's art in far-away Spain.

The mission was the social center of a wide area. It consisted of a church, sacristy, and baptistry. Besides these, there were shops for the industries such as weaving, hat, shoe and rug making, carpentry, blacksmithing, soap and candle making, great store houses for hides and wools and grain, a house for the Abbot, a hospital and

---

*"In and Out of the Old Missions of California." George Wharton James. Courtesy of Little Brown and Company.

guest rooms. It was the same old plan that the Benedictines had used in the old world. There is the same patio enclosed by a protecting wall or lined with shops. In the cloisters the padres walked and meditated, as the sound of the crafts came from within. In the courts children of the natives played or came to school to be taught the stories of the Christ Child, and the women filled their water jugs from the well as in the Orange Court at Cordova.

San Juan de Capistrano, partially destroyed by earthquake, is a most picturesque ruin, with its great Romanesque arches and vast blank walls on which the shadows cast today pictures as beautiful as they did in the garden of the Alcazar. The gardens of the Santa Barbara Mission are still kept up and I imagine the monks continue to make their cordials and medicines. From the three little niches in their towers, the bells still call the faithful to prayer.

The golden days of the Mission lasted from 1800 to 1813. Padre Serra, having fought a good fight and established a spiritual and temporal domain for the King of Spain, died in 1785. The missions prospered and became wealthy estates absolutely and solely administered by the padres, who were not only the preachers of the country, but also its great farm managers, its great merchants, and so far as the Indian population was concerned, its rulers.

Our garden way has brought us to the Golden Gate. Again we see the sun set in the ocean and underneath it lies the East. Boats ply back and forth from China, the land of Punt where three thousand years ago Queen Hatshepsut found the incense trees for her terraced gardens. Over our heads tower the redwood trees, and scientists tell us they have been growing seven thousand years and were old in the time of Hatshepsut. Well might they stand as symbols of the tree of life. Where did the seeds come from?

One theory is that Noah brought them. Another that once a great continent lay in the Pacific between our country and China.

CHAPTER VIII

THE PATH FROM WEST TO EAST

CHAPTER VIII

As the nineteenth century dawns we turn away from the Golden Gate and gaze across the country around which we have traveled. A new nation is born, Colonial days are over, but as yet no road connects the East and West. However, by the middle of the century the Indian trails have opened up the way for the covered wagon to bring adventurers from the East seeking gold in the West. Many became discouraged on the long trail and made homes for themselves along the way. Opportunities opened up, and great cities were born. Agriculture, the backbone of civilization, blossomed into horticulture and landscape gardeners threw themselves into the work of building a new country.

Andrew Jackson Downing in 1846 edited the Horticulturist in which he advocated the natural style of landscape work, which became immensely popular. He was followed by Frederick Law Olmstead, Senior, who was born in Hartford, Connecticut, in 1822, and died in Brookline in 1903. His real work as landscape architect began in 1857, when he was appointed superintendent of the New Central Park in New York City. The work then under construction was stopped by the Civil War but later resumed under his care. He soon became in great demand all over the country. With him was associated Calvert Vaux, a capable English-trained architect, formerly the partner of Downing. Olmstead was the first man in America to organize and practice the profession of landscape architects on a large scale. He had associated with him a number of young men, his two sons among them. His influence was exerted through his disciples and his works, which extended widely through Canada and the United States. This period might well be called the park era.

His principles are: (1) Preserve the natural scenery and, if necessary, restore and emphasize it; (2) avoid all formal design except in very limited areas about buildings; (3) keep open lawns and meadows in large central areas; (4) use native trees and shrubs, especially in heavy border plantings; (5) provide circulation by means of paths and roads laid in wide-sweeping curves; (6) place the principal road so that it will approximately circumscribe the whole area. Park cemeteries were laid out, and this is a distinct American contribution to landscape architecture.

Neighborhood playgrounds followed, then park reservations and country clubs for recreation, until now the whole country is linked up by National Parks, National Forests, National Monuments, state parks, state forests and local parks.

All through the Olmstead period flower beds flourished. Round beds filled with Canna vied with hot Salvia in masses; scrolls of Colea were spread on the lawn, taking the place of the mediaeval knots of clipped green. Even in these flower-bed-days, there were lovely gardens of sweet-smelling flowers. Memories of the garden of my childhood days come out of the mist and I recall the three terraces of my grandfather's old garden, separated from ours by a driveway. On one of the terraces grew daffodils and sweet-scented violets, to be had for the picking. At the end of the path by the old well grew a rose of great beauty, which I remember well, though its name is gone. In our garden my mother cherished a moss rose from her old home in Keene, New Hampshire. Over the side piazza grew the Baltimore Belle and Prairie Rose by the side of white Jessamine and honeysuckle. A border of sweet-scented white clover gave me the contents of many a scent bag for my grandmother's Christmas present. An old box tree was my chariot, a lilac bush my doll house. Under a weeping ash, I kept house; from a willow tree my swing carried me to the clouds; the leafing of the Copper Beech was an annual event.

Probably to please the gardener there were Canna and Colea but I do not remember them. There must have been magenta petunias somewhere for I have always fought petunia in our garden until now the hybrids have captivated me.

Conservatory and glass house came with prosperity. There old Dennis taught me the art of lifting the seedlings and potting them, and now as I do it, his admonition rings in my ears, "Firm it down, Miss, firm it down."

After the Olmstead period came a delightful revival of Colonial art. Fashions change but old ones come back.

The covered wagon no longer exists; the path has broadened into a highway for motors, but truly a garden way thousands of miles long. Through California stretch miles of yellow poppies; acres of blue lupin spread the sky at our feet. Fields are like a mosaic pavement with millions of tiny flowers; the mist of wild lilac covers the hillsides; the air is laden with the perfume of orange blossoms. The canyons are full of beauty and from some sheltered spot the Mariposa lily lifts its queenly head. Across the desert the cacti color the sands; the mimosa and acacia fill the air with fragrance. The swamps of Texas are blue with iris. The Judas tree and gum trees brighten the dismal swamp through which the coastal highway brings us north. Through the southland the citrus orchards rival those in California.

Acres and acres are pink with peach orchards in Georgia and Carolina. Creeks open through the swamp land to hidden lakes where the white heron nests in the midst of the blue-green Lotus leaves with their opalescent blossoms, the Egyptian lily of fire and water, the symbol of creation used so extensively in Egyptian art, especially as the attribute of Osiris. The Hindoos used it too as a symbol of creative power, the Greeks and Romans as a symbol of resurrection, while in Christian times it becomes the lily of the Virgin; and in the form of the iris the Florentines have made it the emblem of the state. Here in southern swamps it grows wild for the alligator and the heron. One of these wild swamps has been cleared and opened up as the Cypress Garden, and undoubtedly the lotus will be seen there under the little Chinese bridges that connect island to island in the midst of the gigantic cypress trees towering out of the black water.

Trees festooned with yellow jessamine mingling with the mysterious Spanish moss add an unique charm to the way, culminating in the indescribable magnolia gardens which must be seen before one dies. The Spanish moss is a most mysterious air plant. Great masses hang by a tiny thread to the live oak by preference, and rarely touch a nearby pine. It follows the tidal rivers about thirty miles inland and suddenly stops. As the tide comes in, the long moss-veils wave in rhythmic sympathy and constantly suggested to me the old mammies' swaying bodies as they sang lullabies to their piccaninnies— or as the wind rose, suggested the emotional Spirituals. As we journeyed north, the ground, under crepe-myrtle bushes, gleamed with the narcissus; wistaria festooned the trees and houses. Up the Ashley River many old plantations still stand. On the Middleton estate the live oaks have grown into gigantic trees, but rice fields are no more. Over long deserted homesteads the Spanish moss throws its mystic veil.

The old church of Jamestown is now a national shrine, a temple wreathed in ivy standing in a grove. Williamstown is being rapidly reconstructed into its old-time charm, a monument of Colonial days. All along the James river many lordly mansions are still lived in by the descendants of Colonial days, who generously opened their grounds and houses for the Virginia Garden Club's great enterprise in restoring Gen. Lee's old home. I felt myself indeed fortunate to have had the privilege of visiting them, the memory of which will be treasured through my life. The little Westover Church on the hill above the estate with a flock of sheep browsing around it still stands loved by its parish. All through Tidewater Virginia, these estates bear witness of the charm of England's Colonies.

The path to the North takes us through the Shenandoah Valley with its apple trees in bloom, its dogwood, azalea, rhododendrons running through Pennsylvania and New Jersey, where once the dog tooth violet and columbine were common. In New England there is still a quantity of laurel. Lady slippers and arbutus are not all exterminated as yet in this machine age. Our bogs are full of rare orchids, the joy of botanists. Each season brings its treasures; elderberry, meadow rue, fire weed, field lilies, Jo Pie weed, asters, Cardinal flower, and last but not least, the rare fringed gentian and witch hazel. Poets have immortalized them all. From May to November there is a succession of color. In October the trees and bushes are glorious, and when November comes the pines are greener than ever and the tracery of the leafless trees most beautiful of all.

The society for the conservation of wild flowers is doing a noble work, especially in the schools. Garden clubs have sprung up like mushrooms. Linked together in state federations or united in the Garden Club of America, they are wielding a wide influence in the improvement of the countryside from Maine to California. A great menace to our beauty spots, however, lies in the widening of our country roads, making them straight in order that motors may rush through at greater speed than ever. The charming wood roads that once were Indian trails! What can we do to stop it?

On a recent visit to three gardens within the radius of a mile, I saw in the first a broad and beautiful Italian terrace as a foreground to Mount Monadnock, while a series of terraced gardens led down to enchanting enclosures where every kind of flower found a home.

The second garden was on a level with the house and suggested the "giardino secreto" where the ladies of mediaeval days worked as garden lovers do today. As in the first garden visited, here the broad lawn leads the eye to Monadnock against which stand out giant pines as sentinels guarding the old monarch.

The third garden, was a museum of gardens filled with delightful relics of the past, collected by the owner who also himself made reproductions most cleverly. An Italian angel presided in a garden of columns and flowers from which a path led to a tiny theatre in overgrown verdure with the air of antiquity about it; beyond, the path led by still waters to a large amphitheatre where the stage, framed with classic columns, suggests a Greek drama, against a background of water. Chinese symbolism has found a place in an unique porch full of Chinese treasures and terrifying monsters. Bordering the lake, a Japanese garden with its labyrinth of stones and clipped firs, tiny pagodas and lanterns, brings Japan to New Hampshire.

Modernists are introducing a new garden architecture where growing plants are conspicuous by their absence. Checker boards pave an enclosure in symmetrical patterns. Stone pavements take the place of velvet lawns. Over them falls the tracery of vines and trellises, making charming pictures at our feet; but this so-called modern movement is not new. All these features were tried out in many lands long before our day of modernism, which is just a new fashion and, many of us trust, a passing one. A few years ago there was a craze for enlarging flowers; now the new fad is to reduce them to miniature. Old-time knotted beds of green are revived in geometrical designs of low-growing bordered beds. Roof gardens recall the Adonis gardens of Greek days. Here Moorish mosaic architecture can be used with good effect and shallow beds are not so bad. Shadows from covered galleries even on cement floors are rather pleasing, and help one bear the odium of city life. The modern pent house is a treasure, and the transformation of the ugly city back yard into an Eastern courtyard is a fascinating problem to many an artist.

Like England our country is a land of homes. Every known style of architecture has its vogue in America. While we copy we are not bound to tradition but are learning to combine harmoniously architecture and landscape. Landscape architecture has become an overcrowded profession; schools are sending out trained workers and ever since the fifteenth century, literature has been plentiful and today is overwhelming. Even seed catalogues are works of art. M. Forestier, the great French landscape architect, tells us that there are three essentials in a garden,—color, fragrance, and privacy. We have found these in all eastern gardens where we found water also an essential. The four sides of the enclosure were the symbols of these essentials. Throughout the East we have found the symbolism of religion also an important feature in the gardens. In our American gardens there is very little thought given to this fascinating subject delightfully told in a little book by Elizabeth Goldsmith.

We forget that our terraced gardens are the descendants of the holy hills of Pagan days. George Russell in his delightful book "Song and Its Fountains" says that the "Mount is a symbol for that peak of soul, when, gone inward into itself, it draws nigh to its own divine root, and memory and imagination are shot through and through with the radiance of another nature."* The quotation brings to my mind a friend's garden on the side of a hill, in which stands a small statue of St. Francis by a tiny fountain where the birds drink in the midst of old time flowers.

I recall a garden of another friend where Pan pipes to those who listen in a rose garden of rare charm. Symbolism is finding a place in our gardens.

My sister and I have a little garden terraced on a New England hillside. As the granite steps lead up, there is set in the wall the Franciscan motto, "Pax et Bonum." Above stand two Sicilian pine cones, the emblem of Sicilian hospitality. In the little garden are roses and lilies loved by the Virgin, a pool reflects the sky and seats invite one to linger.

As a path leads up to the woods, a simple wayside shrine shelters a seventeenth century Madonna. Perhaps it sounds a little pretentious and inappropriate; on the contrary it is very simple and carries a message.

---

*Song and Its Fountains. A. E. (George Russell). Courtesy of Macmillan Co.

Its creator loves it. Evolved from her own ideas, without the help of landscape architect, it possesses all the essentials with the added charm of mountain background, and expresses the thought of Mr. Russell again.

"Beyond form, the creator; beyond thought, the thinker;
Behind intuition, the seer."

Our garden way might have ended at the Golden Gate or taken us to Point Loma where the Eastern tradition still has its devoted followers living there in a garden of beauty, facing the Pacific Ocean; but the law of attraction has swung us back in a great curve to the Atlantic and has brought us to Mount St. Albans where, above our Capitol, is slowly rising our national cathedral. Like the temples of old, it stands in a grove of trees where the Preachers' College carries on the tradition of the ancient academies. In the midst of its group of Gothic structures there is a little cloister, thirty feet square, where a hundred-year-old wistaria, an ancient yew, and a long-neglected magnolia are now renewing their youth around a fountain made of an old grinding stone surrounded with a circle cut from one huge block of granite. A tiny jet throws high its spray of water, mingling delightfully with the light and shade of this quiet spot reserved for the meditation of preachers seeking inspiration.

A path leads down to the Bishop's garden, enclosed by a wall under which runs a border of perpetual bloom, the plants of which are the gifts of friends and clubs from far and near. Little steps lead up and down, through box-bordered flower-beds where every plant speaks of the friend from whom it came. Roses of every age and color are charmingly planted; in the midst of them a capital from a thirteenth century ruined monastery near

Rheims now marks the time of day as a sun dial. Stone copings about the beds have come from the quarry where George Washington worked himself; bricks from Nellie Custis's home pave the walks. From early Christian days a wheel cross again raises here the symbol of the Christian faith.

Mrs. Bratenahl is in charge of the landscape design and development. Her story is an interesting tale of adventure and untiring effort and gives us a splendid example of the evolution of a garden from a rough hillside. Mrs. Bratenahl tells how, having completed the Bishop's garden, after three years of intensive effort, she was resting in the garden after the excitement of the General Convention had passed, thinking how lovely and restful it was. Suddenly as she looked beyond the wayside cross there dawned upon her the vision of the Pilgrim steps. Within a month she had made the design and submitted it to the chapter and architects. Her faith and courage were rewarded by generous donors and the dream became a reality. Through the splendid co-operation and enthusiasm of the workers, "the conscious stone to beauty grew" and now the garden way climbs the hill, over a Norman bridge, past an open-air auditorium to the Pilgrim steps, a perfect path for the great processions that ascend to the temple.

At the foot of the steps the design includes an iron gate bearing a scroll on which is wrought, "They shall enter into peace that enter in at these gates." Peace? Not that of an Oriental Monarch! Rather the peace of a Mrs. Bratenahl to whom from the quiet of the cloister opened a vision of greater effort beyond the garden wall.

The four essentials of plant life become the symbols of human life; effort, inspiration, enthusiasm, sincerity. Without these no garden ever becomes a reality. Dreams and fancies carry us to the rainbow arch, the Indian's path to Paradise, from whence, perchance, we may come in Demeter's dragon-fly chariot to scatter seeds along the garden way of fellowship from North to South, from East to West.

> "In miracles of fire
> He symbols forth his days,
> In dreams of crystal light
> Reveals what pure pathways
> Lead to the soul's desire,
> The silence of the height."
>
> A. E.